Married to Mayhem

My Journey, Memories and Struggles
of
Coping with a BPD Loved One

Berkeley Carson

Table of Contents

Foreword   1

Definition   3

The Email   6

Acorns Make Trees 13

Habits of Bad Choices   23

Lying, Thieving   31

The Manipulation   41

Her New Weapons 51

Female Wars   60

Wrestling, George and Promiscuity   67

My Buttons Are Pushed   74

The Light Is Turned On   83

Drugs Don't Make It Better   93

The Last Chance   100

Incomplete Hail Mar   106

What I Learned   111

About the Author   120

Foreword

I have never written a book and am not a licensed Psychiatrist, or any other mental health professional. My qualifications include an undergraduate degree in Psychology along with several years of in depth research and reading looking for answers to answer why I was in my situation. I've also had many years of individual psychotherapy. But, everyone knows when something just isn't right even if they can't solve the problems. I wrote this book to share my story of what it is like to have a relationship with someone who I believe has Borderline Personality Disorder.

October 7, 2012: one day after our six year anniversary. I sat alone with all four children as my second wife, Jessica, is supposedly over at her friend's house (where she has decided to move). I wasn't really sure if she was with her friend, spending time with some else or out on the town. But it was the day that I made my final decision to divorce her.

In order to protect identity of everyone, I have changed the names, locations and certain details around events. I will do my best to deliver all sides of the story and give you an unbiased interpretation — I clearly have my fair share of flaws and feel that they need to be pointed out as well.

I also want to make sure that you understand that I loved my wife and her children more than anything in the world. However, I feel it is important to share my experiences with people who may be in the same situation, need help or might be searching for answers as they face situations similar to my ten year difficult journey.

When I decided to start writing this book, I thought the completion would be rather quick since there were so many situations and circumstances that took place while we were together that impacted the outcome. Much to my dismay, it has been a much longer process than I could have imagined. Between finding enough time to write and the great hurdle of revisiting the thoughts and memories that caused so much heartache and pain, often months would pass without me writing a word simply because it was easier to forget than to repeatedly rip the Band-Aid off the wound.

My hope is that I can help anyone who has been in a similar situation, so they know that there are other people out there just like them. This has been a long ongoing progression of my life, and I look forward in sharing these memories with you. If you have been or feel like you are possibly going down this same road, it might be in your best interest to see how and why my story ended up where it did.

Definition

In this book, I have done my best to describe as accurately as possible the key situations and incidents that transpired throughout this relationship. There were times of great affection and love while other situations seemed to have "high conflict."

You should be aware of the nine characteristics of Borderline Personality Disorder described in the Diagnostic and Statistical Manual of Mental Disorders (or DSM for short), the standard criteria used among the mental health professionals in the United States to classify mental disorders. If you are unaware of the symptoms, here is a quick review of the dimensions that relate to the biological, psychological, social and other aspects of Borderline Personality Disorder (what I shorthand as BPD in the book) in the most current DSM-5.

- Frantic efforts to avoid real or imagined abandonment

- A pattern of unstable and intense interpersonal relationships characterized by alternating between extremes of idealization and devaluation

- Identity disturbance, such as a significant and persistent unstable self-image or sense of self

- Impulsivity in at least two areas that are potentially self-damaging (e.g., spending, sex, substance abuse, reckless driving, binge eating)

- Recurrent suicidal behavior, gestures, or threats, or self-mutilating behavior

- Emotional instability due to significant reactivity of mood (e.g., intense episodic dysphoria, irritability, or anxiety usually lasting a few hours and only rarely more than a few days)

- Chronic feelings of emptiness

- Inappropriate, intense anger or difficulty controlling anger (e.g., frequent displays of temper, constant anger, recurrent physical fights)

- Transient, stress-related paranoid thoughts or severe dissociative symptoms

In order to be diagnosed BPD by a licensed therapist, you must meet five of the nine criteria. Please understand that I am not interested in the label of BPD as a diagnosis, but rather to describe my experiences with my ex-wife along with the actions that occurred. All too often, labels - BPD, Bi-Polar, Narcissism, et cetera - come with a negative connotation. My purpose in sharing our story is to uncover and explain what it is like to live with what I believe to be a BPD (with eight of the nine traits) and helping others who have experienced similar incidents understand that they are not alone.

I can only talk about my actual experiences and know that there are others who have lived with a BPD that turned out better than ours. In my relationship, when things were good they were GREAT, and when there were problems it was HELL. Without a doubt, the problems that transpired were extremely painful and caused me to question my character, my own identity and why I chose to marry this person.

I hope and pray this will provide insight and understanding into what can happen if you are in a relationship or in love with someone who has a borderline personality disorder.

Chapter 1

The Email

In 2001 after being married for 14 years, my life came to an abrupt halt. My wife, Tina, and I had just had our second child. With literally two in diapers, I found out my wife was having an affair. I felt like my entire world had been turned upside down. Though finding out about the affair was completely unexpected, it was still like being hit by a Mack truck going 100 miles per hour. I had learned about the affair not from my wife but from a recording she didn't realize existed; I went home to confront her about what I had heard. At first she denied the affair, but eventually said it was true.

Just to give you an idea of how much this effected my life, I found out about the affair around 8 p.m. on Sunday, September 9, 2001; Tina and I spent the majority of that evening discussing the painful issue. After a restless Sunday and Monday night, I woke and went to work only to discover one of the most horrific events to ever occur in the history of the United States as the twin towers collapsed on Tuesday morning. Sadly, I was completely incoherent and disconnected to America's tragedy. While everyone around the world was glued to their televisions, I would go running, clean the house and stay busy. I am the only person I know that does not remember having felt the effect of this great tragedy of 9/11. I am completely numb to any feeling as I had my own "twin towers" collapsing around me.

I was hopeful that the affair would not break our marriage apart, but within four weeks she informed me that she had made the decision to go her own way. I remember she told me had filed for divorce and the only thing I could think was *I am not going to have a 50th anniversary*. Coming from a religious family-oriented childhood, life was defined by you, your wife and the family. The divorce as absolutely the hardest thing I have ever gone through and I spent the next eight to ten months slowly working through the pain to rebuild myself.

In the summer of 2002, I decided to enter the infamous life of online dating. It was not so much that I was looking for my next wife, but rather the fact that Tina's affair had an effect on my manhood. I had spent an incredible amount of time out partying with my guy friends at the bar scene; however, none of the women ever seemed to match my fantasy. As I reflect now, I was still not ready to have a serious relationship and had probably jaded thoughts about jumping back into a marriage.

In August of that year, I decided to take two members of my staff to Chicago the following month for a trade show and thought *nothing could be better than to have a lady to escort me around the Windy City.* Using my online dating site, I thought I would just change my search area to Chi-town as I hoped to start working on my potential "weekend fling." I figured it would take several weeks to lay the ground work for developing a connection with a woman I'd meet online in order to circumvent any delay to a fun seductive weekend when I arrived. No, please don't throw me into "the player" category; I just needed repair my manhood that was shattered from the affair and then the divorce, with the solution being some much needed attention from a lady to help.

I sent 10 to 12 emails to likely candidates who fit my requirements and looked attractive in their photos. After receiving three responses back from my email outriggers, I spent the next few days exchanging emails with them, deciding who (or if any) I wanted to meet. Hands down, there was no question that this woman named Jessica was my choice. We seemed to have the most common. She also appeared intelligent, attractive, well spoken, had a good career and most of all, was extremely empathic to my needs as we talked on the phone. Hell, I just wanted a of couple days of fun and entertainment. This should be very simple: get off the airplane, have dinner, hit some clubs, come back to my room and if I'm lucky maybe repeat it again the next day. I am in on Friday and out Sunday. What could happen?

Looking back, this was the very moment of aimlessly broadcasting out emails via an internet dating site that would set the wheels in motion for a most happy, exciting, miserable and turbulent rollercoaster part of my life for the next decade. I have thought about this action repeatedly over the past several years and have played the movie in my mind so many times and in so many ways that I sometimes get mad at myself. *What if I would have entered a narrower search in the downtown zip code? What if I would have just looked more closely at her profile and photo? What if she would have been so far down the list I searched that I never came across her profile? What if I just would have entered one more or removed one preference in the search profile? What if? What if?*

I have beaten myself up so many times with these questions. But back to the story. At that second when I wrote the original "looking-in-Chicago" email and pressed send, my life would be changed forever.

Jessica and I spent the next three weeks talking every day and often at night. She told me about her college life, earning her master's degree in Sociology and her general interests, then I shared things about myself. It was comforting that she was bright, educated and in a similar sales field as myself. I really enjoyed having someone listen to me and caring for what I had to say as well as what was happening in my life. Granted, I had been married for 14 years but I had never had someone so "in tune" with my interest. I had been so deprived of this quality that I became almost addicted to our conversations. We would start talking at 7:00 and the next thing I knew it was 11:00. The trip was arriving soon and I looked forward to finally meeting her.

The weekend finally arrived and I was somewhat apprehensive yet excited at the same time. I mean, what the hell? I am in town and if I don't like what I see I will go out and hit the clubs solo. What do I have to lose? I recall seeing the majority of Jessica's pictures from the waist up, which led me to believe she might be on the thicker side, but it didn't matter because this was a one-time deal. Let's be serious. How does a business owner from Kansas City keep a relationship going with someone in Chicago?

I arrived in Chicago on Friday in the late afternoon with my colleagues and we headed for the hotel in the downtown area. On the way in the taxi, I let Jessica know I had landed and would text her to let her know where we could meet. About an hour later, I called to let her know her know I would be ready shortly and I thought we could meet at The Lion, which was my hotel's restaurant. She agreed and I finished getting ready, made my way down to the bar and waited with a cocktail for her arrival. Ten minutes later, I looked up to see a lady who appeared to look like Jessica come through the revolving door. I stood up and in a hesitant tone asked,

"Jessica?" She responded with enthusiasm that it was her, and greeted me with a hug.

We were quickly seated at a table. I was hungry so ordered some food and we got caught up on small talk. She was so easy to talk to, very inquisitive about me and my interests. I had never experienced anything like this and found it very refreshing. As we sat, we held hands across the table and talked about the schedule for the night's activities. I had pulled out all the stops by asking one of my friends who had some connections in Chicago about getting us on "the list" at one of the newest clubs. Jessica appeared impressed as we strolled to the front of the line and gave the doorman my name. He glanced down at his clipboard for a moment, then politely opened the rope allowing us to cruise past the line of people. We spent about 45 minutes there and then I informed her I had us on "the list" at another club as well. We finished our drink and grabbed a cab to hit the next place.

As we entered, the host guided us to a VIP lounge and we found a sofa where we started some hot and heavy making out. She seemed so aggressive in the way she kissed me, almost like a tiger eating their young. I found it much more animalistic than sensual, but was still very turned on. We spent the next few hours engaged between minutes of small talk and making out. I knew at the moment we left the second place that I was going to have a visitor back in my hotel room.

Upon opening my hotel door, I immediately undressed as she went to the bathroom. When finished, Jessica crack the door and ask me to turn off the lights; she said she didn't want me to see her body. Apparently, when Jessica was pregnant in her first marriage, she developed a severe case of toxemia that caused her to gain over 100 pounds. This, along with after effects of stretch marks and sagging skin around her stomach and breast area, made her extremely self-conscious. She felt I might think differently about her, so I gladly obliged then she hopped into bed. In a matter of seconds, her gloves came off.

I thought to myself, "Wow, this girl is into some Jurassic Park sex." If there would have been rafters, we would have been hanging from them. She said, "Fuck me harder," repeatedly and asked me to pull her hair. Half way through the animalistic frenzy, Jessica exclaimed, "let's get rid of this" and reached down and ripped off my condom. Hell, I had not experienced anything like this my entire life. It was a guy's dream come true. No love making tonight, just raw fucking. We spent the next hour doing virtually everything I had fantasized about to a woman. When the night ended, I escorted her to her car and thanked her for a wonderful evening when she asked, "What are you doing tomorrow?" I told her I would call in the morning and give her my schedule.

I did call the following day and told her that I had made reservations for my staff and I to eat downtown and she was more than welcome to drop by. After discussions about her not wanting to intrude and me assuring her I would enjoy seeing her again, she agreed to stop at the restaurant. As I sat with my work colleagues that night for dinner, towards the end of the meal Jessica showed up and I introduce her to everyone. I am sure they knew that Jessica and I were going to go hit the town once again. That night was basically a carbon copy of the previous night: clubs, drinks and more crazy-ass sex. I thought I had died and gone to heaven! As the night ended moved into morning, she knew I was leaving that day and wanted to have breakfast. I agreed, especially since she had been so accommodating.

We ate before I asked her if she could drop me back at the hotel. She agreed and we hopped in her car for a quick three minute drive. We pulled in front of the building, taking a few minutes of doing that "civil thing" where you say nice comments to someone from a weekend fling while knowing you will probably never each other see again.

I got out of the car, gave her a hug and kiss when she drops, "I really enjoyed meeting you and would like to see you again." All I remember is thinking to myself, *What is she thinking?* She continued to share that "she did not have her kids next weekend and would like to fly down and see me." Holy Shit, this was supposed to be a turn and burn deal; now she wants to fly down to Kansas City. I offhandedly tell her something like "sure that would be great" while thinking that it was lip service. IT WAS NOT! Jessica called Monday to tell me she had already made flight reservations to come and see me. Wow, this girl moves lightning fast. Now that's impulsive.

It started with just an email!

Chapter 2

Acorns Make Trees

Her flight landed the following weekend as I waited in the terminal as a chauffeur would, with a sheet of paper with her name "JESSICA" printed on it. Even though I knew it seemed a little cheesy, I thought she would find some humor with it, which she did. Everything picked up right like the previous weekend. Wonderful in depth talks, taking her out on the town and (of course) lots and lots of sex. From the time she landed at 7:00 p.m. on Friday until her departure at 2:00 p.m. on Sunday, we had sex a total of nine times. I found myself starting to slowly connect with Jessica; she was a lot of fun. I enjoyed her companionship and physical connection. She made me feel good about myself, so it just made sense that when her initial visit ended we talk about when we might see each other again.

We both spent the next several months flying back and forth between Chicago and Kansas City. Every weekend either she was in KC or I was in Chicago. There was not a day that we didn't talk on the phone for at least an hour and sometimes more. It was during the first few months I that I began to see and learn about Jessica's childhood along with the relationship with her parents. She shared numerous stories about how her parents neglected and mistreated her while she was younger, which left me feeling sorry for her. It was difficult to comprehend everything she told me, since I was lucky to have two wonderful parents who loved, nurtured and guided me as a child through adolescence.

It was on my third visit to Chicago that I had my first contact with Jessica's mother, Dora. My initial reaction was how there was such a lack of warmth between the two women. Both expressed little affection towards each other though there was a slight amount of bantering. I couldn't relate to this and immediately considered *if this is the way Jessica treats her mother, how would she treat me?* On the other hand, I could tell that Dora only cared about herself and since Jessica was an extension of her, she felt it was her obligation to provide her daughter with her beliefs and point of views.

After a half an hour of visiting, I could easily see how difficult it must have been for Jessica to have any type of positive relationship with her own mother. Dora's smug arrogant aura left me with a strong feeling of not wanting to spend any more time around the lady and really did not care if I met her again.

Jessica's upbringing was one of my biggest areas of concern while dating and yet I chose to overlook what I felt was an important characteristic for a companion. I did this most likely for two reasons: first, she made me feel like I was the most important person in the world. With BPD individuals, they work back and forth between idealization and devaluation. Clearly Jessica had me feeling like I was "King of the Mountain." Having someone dote on you and give you everything you need both emotionally and physically is very intoxicating. I had never been treated this way and chose to drown myself in the pool of admiration. Secondly, that damn sex played a strong factor in the early stages. The combination of idealization and passionate sex together was an euphoric cocktail that in the beginning was great, yet would crumble over time.

In the majority of cases, BPD people often are deprived from the love and nurturing in their childhood and for Jessica, that was no exception though I didn't realize how strongly it would play in our own relationship years later. Having two nurturing parents is ideal; however, for a young girl I believe that a positive father figure is very important. Jessica's father (George) grew up in an extremely dysfunctional family in rural Tennessee. He was an only child and his father was very abusive to both him and his mother. Over the years, he grew very resentful towards his father due to his constant drinking, philandering and physical as well as emotion abuse. His parents would go back and forth with many problems over the years (including them divorcing and remarrying each other three times due from his father's abuse).

As George passed through his late teens and into young adulthood, there were many physical altercations between him and his father over the treatment of his mother. He had been witness to so much violence, criticism and lack of love that his character formed a foundation for what he became and how he viewed the world. He knew nothing about empathy and was a hard, coarse, antisocial individual. Later in life after George had grown into adulthood, his father had an epiphany that caused him to stop drinking, becoming a better person and husband. However, George's personality had already been formed and he enlisted in the military, ultimately ending up the higher ranks of the Green Berets.

The Army allowed George to travel the world in a structured environment. Combined with Special Forces training and ideology, he felt a strong sense of patriotism, allegiance and entitlement. (In fact, his extreme devotion had not changed to the last time I saw him in 2010.) There is no difference between the days where he engaged in battle and if you ran into him at the grocery store. He absolutely bleeds Red, White and Blue.

I remember Jessica describing her father as a cold hearted, non-empathic person who was extremely opinionated, prejudiced and kept most people at arm's length. But her description was a reflection of how she saw him, too, as a result of how their relationship was formed. The fact that people stayed away because of George's attitudes was really not a problem, since most people in their town were somewhat intimated of him and would rather not be around him. In high school, Jessica's classmate gave him the nickname "Rambo" after the character Sylvester Stallone played in the movies during the early 1980's. Stallone plays a man who has trouble distinguishing between "honor" he learned during the Vietnam War and the current real life issues in a post-war community. Sly is truly one "bad ass" and struggles to adapt in a functional civilian life. Similarly, George showed little compassion among people and was of the opinion that there is only one way of thinking; his way!

While stationed in Greece, he ran into a young lady named Dora, who lived in Athens with her parents. Both are captivated with one another and spent all of their time together before George was sent back to the United States. Their persistence to continue dating did not stop as they spent the next year writing letters back and forth. Finally, Dora makes the decision to leave her home country of Greece and make the journey to the United States to live with her American Casanova. Unbeknownst to her, George was then living in a small town of ten thousand in rural northeast Illinois, which would be a drastic change from the enormous Athens to which she has been accustomed.

Her mother was the youngest of two. Her own father was very verbally abusive towards her and had a set of double standards for Dora's only brother. Their dad provided little (if any) nurturing, direction, love or compassion towards her brother, mother or her. From stories, the man was full of criticism towards her and I never heard her talk about any overtures of love from her mother. My gut tells me that Jessica's grandfather - Dora's father - is the strong male type while the grandmother is a passive individual who never challenges her husband. I am sure this leaves Dora with no sense of worth or esteem throughout her entire childhood and into her early twenties. The lack of nurturing and love from her father even continues later in life when Dora and Jessica return to Europe to visit. Jessica shared with me on one occasion that she recalled her grandfather commenting about them staying out late one evening by saying "only whores stay out til that time of night."

Given this background, I can only image of what Dora was thinking when her knight in shining armor picked her up at the busy Chicago airport and escorted her out to the corn fields of Illinois, which likely started tainting her personality from day one. I am sure she had the idea that she would be able to look out of windows and view the skyscrapers of Chicago; instead, she was in the middle of rural Illinois looking at cows and farmland. The courting period is rather short before they choose to get married, and not long thereafter Jessica was born. I have seen several pictures of both parents and Jessica from that time and they all appear to be a normal, young, happy family with excitement about their new infant.

Unfortunately, the pictures I have seen were ones just like almost every parent has when they have a new child enter the world. The birth of a new child (especially the first baby) is filled with elation and freshness to a family. However in this case, the excitement is short lived. Jessica's adolescence years are not much better than either George's or Dora's.

The lack of quality parental guidance and nurturing helps form a very narcissistic environment combined with lack of respect for virtually anyone. Dora continued to pass down all the negative things she had learned from her father, constantly bitching and complaining to Jessica (or anyone else that will listen). One characteristic of Dora's narcissism can be referred to as "accomplished narcissism," where she is only concerned with people who have wealth, power or are well-educated. For her, it is more important about the type of car you drive or balance of your checking account than your character. It has always been very important to Dora that Jessica to be involved with someone who is up to her standards — and she has made that well known over the years even though Dora has no money, no power and is uneducated herself.

Jessica's parents got divorced, sadly after only five years; Dora was faced with an enormous amount of turmoil. Being uneducated, foreign and somewhat difficult to understand her speech due to a strong accent, there was little demand for her in the work force. Combine that with George refusing to pay child support and there was a recipe for a very low income experience. Jessica spent most of her childhood in a small apartment with little amenities and no family car. I had listened to Jessica many times talk about the humiliation of always having to ask friends for a ride to and from school, where so many times she resorted to lying about why or how she needed a ride home. She also would not have money for lunch and would sometimes steal food from the cafeteria or make up some excuse for being penniless so she could mooch from another friend.

The lying becomes a common occurrence in the everyday transportation escapades. Manipulation is learned at an early age, which held true in Jessica's case, so she could get what she needed for survival and self-preservation. The pressure of how she was viewed by peers and her survival was (and is) extraordinary for a child or young teenager.

I truly cannot imagine the feeling and anxiety Jessica had daily with normal routines. The pressure of having to survive in school, creating friendships and portraying a normal home-life has to be so extreme for an adolescent. Combine that with a young lady that has to constantly be ashamed of her "crazy European mom," the woman who had to give her outspoken opinion to anyone and everyone. During our relationship, Jessica would talk about the embarrassment she had as a child with the way she felt and how she saw others act around her mother. This was a tremendous burden for a young woman to bare. Dora provided no loving, teaching or guidance, and would often leave Jessica alone for several days - even up to a week while she traveled for work or going off with her new husband. Her mother appeared to have no regard for leaving her alone any circumstance. The only thing her mother cared about is her needs and desires. Fear of abandonment is one of major symptoms of a BPD and Dora did an excellent job of helping her child feel this way.

Dora would chew at Jessica's confidence, spirit and soul. Yet, she wouldn't help her improve what she saw as "flaws." Dora would complain at how Jessica thinned her eyebrows and shame her attempts at being woefully inadequate as compared to the beautiful American celebrities like Brooke Shields. But when you think about it, why would it be any different than exactly how Dora's father treated her?

A daughter of a narcissistic mother most often can identify that her mom has has no empathy towards her child. Dora couldn't exhibit this quality because she never saw it growing up and I am sure she finds it is difficult to do something she doesn't know how to do. She has no real connection with Jessica and there is absolutely no understanding of what unconditional love means. The mother-child bond is not only null and void, but seems to be lost in translation with Dora still trying to figure out the American culture in Jessica's early years. To me this is one of the saddest parts — not having the comprehension of what children should receive from their mother (such as love) ends up giving inadequate substitutes that permeate the rest of their life; in this case for Jessica, her "example" of the foundation in a relationship was usually shame.

There was a slow change during her early teen years, where Jessica was forced to be in a parental/child role reversal with her mother (as her father was absent most of the time). Since Dora took no initiative in trying to educate or improve herself, she was always depending on Jessica and friends to provide the simplest task. Jessica would struggle when Dora would leave her alone regularly and in her own mind, this was a manifestation of abandonment prevalent and easy to see. At one point as a teenager, she saw her only escape was to take a whole bottle of aspirin — and then, it was her father, not her mother, at her bedside in the hospital.

While her father could have taken some of the pressure away from her relationship with her mother, she was scared to death of him. Even her ability at sports - which allowed her to get a scholarship to a very expensive school for free - was not enough to build a relationship with him. The only impact was how her achievements would make him look, as he was the father of "The Superstar Athlete." Ironically, he possessed the ability of being very charismatic with people when it came to making a living, and was a successful car salesman even if Jessica never saw any support from those financial achievements.

Toward the end of high school, her continued success in sports drove a wedge between her and her father, as he became an overbearing father constantly pushing her to improve her times and skills. Instead of encouraging her, it was always delivered in negative manner. "You have to work harder. Second place is for losers." She was drilled as he had been drilled. Verbally, he repeatedly she "must be number one." The fear of letting her father's retribution forced her to work harder because it is far easier to go through the practices of blood, sweat and tears than get the abuse from her father. Unfortunately in the later years of high school she injured her ACL, which diminished her value in her father's sight after Division I universities lost interest in her abilities. Her unusual high tolerance to pain though recovering from the surgery made her briefly appear stronger in her father's eyes. I believe that the pain of letting her father down is much greater than any agony she might have felt in her knee.

During my research for this book, one characteristic of the BPD person is a higher degree of pain threshold. The physical pain for a BPD will often be muted by their emotional pains, leaving them with an internal numbness. Within themselves is an inner civil war between the heart aches from the past that then tries to be expressed via suppressing physical bodily sensors in an effort to cover past emotional injury. I really didn't put much thought into it during our courting days when Jessica mentioned how she was able to handle extreme high degrees of pain. She talked about trips to the dentist with no anesthetic and even the birth of Jake and Ian with her first husband being less uncomfortable than she anticipated. (Now it makes perfect sense why she has little suffering in those instances.)

Jessica was not only faced with a barrage of dysfunctional parenting that stifled her emotional development, but also the shame and embarrassment of the perception of her family. She clearly knew and heard from her friends about how her parents were perceived, which effected how she viewed herself. Her prescriptive continues to be "if my parents are socially impaired, then I must be as well." She dealt with peer pressures of having few material items due to finances - even going so far as to living out of a car because her mother could not afford an apartment, then being forced to sell the car in order to move into low income housing.

By her teenage years, the cards were being dealt for Jessica's self-perception for the rest of her life. With no nurturing and no love, abandonment with constant criticism, lack of empathy or guidance, she undoubtedly had been dealt a very shitty hand. I knew that there were people and families like Jessica's out there, but had never been this close to one. My lack of experience affected my misunderstanding in how Dora's background influenced Jessica's behavior. It was not perfect at my household while growing up, but there was constant love and nurturing from both mom and dad that helped build the foundation of who I am.

Chapter 3

Habits of Bad Choices

We continued our long distance relationship into 2003. I liked the setup simply because Jessica was far enough away that I felt no reason to have an exclusive relationship due to distance and the freshness of my divorce. I continued to halfheartedly see other women in Kansas City but enjoyed her attention and the luxury of having my physical needs taken care of on the weekends. It is almost like having a "friend with benefits" with no strings attached. It was very clear to me that Jessica was putting more effort into us seeing each other than I was in the first several months, but I slowly found myself wading deeper into the river of emotional attachment.

I enjoyed the fact that we could talk about anything; it was much different than my previous marriage. Jessica and I spent time discussing our feeling, dreams, childhood and previous marriages. I found it refreshing to be so open. One evening on the phone, she starts telling me that she had not talked with her father in close to 13 years, in spite of recent attempts to make contact with him. She was unable to find his address, but had heard that George was working for the father of a friend. She knew her friend's father from her childhood and called to see if she could get her father's address. The gentleman was rather reluctant to give her the information (knowing George's temperament), but finally gave it to her. Shortly after getting the address, she wrote a long letter that included where she lived, stuff about her job, her phone number and most importantly that he had two wonderful grandsons. The letter was sent and within a week, another envelope arrived with her unopened letter inside of the larger one and a note stating that he did not want to talk to or hear from her.

I should have learned more from another story she shared, too. I knew that Jessica had been through a lot with her ex-husband, but one evening she described issues in great detail. I was amazed at what she told me. She met Joe (her ex-husband) a few years after getting her master's degree and they were married within six months. Dora was opposed to her choice of husband, (of course, since in her opinion she should only be marring someone with wealth and prestige like a doctor or lawyer). Jessica tells me in this story that part of the reason she picked Joe was almost out of spite towards her mother.

Anyway, Joe worked as a finance manager at a car dealership where it was not common to work 90 hours a week. Besides going out every night to drink beer after work, he quickly got involved in sports betting, rapidly finding himself over his head in debt of $25,000 with his bookie calling repeatedly asking when he is going to pay. Joe doesn't have the cash and is forced to flee to Iowa for his supposed safety. Jessica follows her man for six months, but finds being in a mid-sized town in Iowa was depressing (ringing so similar to Dora's experience decades earlier). She decides to leave in part because she couldn't find a good job and once back in Chicago, Joe shortly follows. Still being a wanted man, the bookie there threatening both of their lives. She is force to live in fear not knowing what might happen next. It was all very similar to the life with her mother and the life of her mother - always being afraid of being abandoned or discovered for being truly poor by her friends over lunch money issues, but I didn't see any of this at the time, how her life choices kept replaying themselves.

She tells me that Joe is eventually able to get the money repaid with a loan from his dad, giving her a sense of relief. Her husband decides to change careers, entering the thriving business of mortgage brokering (where he does very well). Finally having some financial structure, they choose to have their first child, whom they name Ian. From the outside, they appear to be like in young couple with their first child; however, Joe continues his betting and drinking with work colleagues. Shortly after their second son, Jake, is born, Joe is rarely home to help with the boys. Her story includes pictures of her bruised torso where Joe hit her when they went out to a concert with friends. Again, it's all shocking to me, seeing and hearing about how much she and the kids had endured and that they are forced into bankruptcy. That's when Jessica mades the decision to file for divorce from Joe, in late 2000.

Jessica took some time to herself and the kids, but in 2001 she was ready to date again, as that seemingly helped her define herself and filled the missing pieces of her life. Entering into the dating world with children can be a delicate deal. I think that adults often bring a companion around kids too soon, so when the relationship ends the kids may be left an empty feeling (especially if they have developed some type of attachment to the person). I had not crossed this bridge with my own kids from my first marriage let alone considered meeting her kids, and wanted to make sure it was handled properly. Both sets of children had already gone through the turmoil of their parents getting divorced and really, I think there should be type of foundation and security where kids can hang their hat. My ex-wife had already brought her lover into the mix and I did not want to exacerbate the issue with my own weekend activities.

I was the first person Jessica really dated after her divorce from Joe and after several months of long distance dating in the early part of 2002, I thought about meeting her children for a while after she mentioned it; I eventually agreed. The following weekend, I flew to Chicago and when she got me at the airport, later that night I met Ian (who was five) and Ian (then three). Still somewhat apprehensive about the introduction, I threw myself into the moment and just had fun with the kids and Jessica. It wasn't a few weeks later when Jessica came to Kansas City and had the opportunity to meet Jeremy and Aspen, my children. She seemed so caring towards my children; it made me feel good. The thought of quite a crew with the kids all close in age (2, 3, 4 and 5) was a bit overwhelming, but I was hopeful about the direction of our relationship.

In spite of my continued concerns, we took the next step and met halfway in St. Louis with all of the children. This was a sensitive situation and I wanted to make sure it was handled correctly. I didn't think we were close enough to the point of having the kids see us sleeping together, so we got adjoining rooms and she slept with her kids and I did the same. We did kid-friendly touristy things locally, and then a few weeks later she decided to fly to Orlando to "help" me with my vacation with Jeremy and Aspen. I didn't question her intentions, but there were flags again: one, why within the first three months she wanted to take off work; two, why spend money flying to Orlando along with two small children, and; three, why was she injecting herself into my family life. I didn't ask her, but certainly enjoyed the attention and help.

It was right after Disneyland in early spring of 2003 when we decided to become exclusive with our relationship. Her admiration of me (i.e. wild sex) was still in full swing and I continued to love how it makes me feel. I am consumed by her idealization of me the next several months. This is probably one of the main reasons (along with the intimacy) that I still continued to see her even though she was 500 miles away. I had no idea that her pendulum could swing as far in the other direction of devaluation down the road, but would clearly find out later.

I have a curveball thrown at me in April of that spring. Jessica happens to mention on the phone one evening that her company has decided to open an office in Minneapolis and one in Kansas City; they are looking for a manager for each spot. Before she can get the words out of her month, I can see where this is going. She is taking my temperature on where I think our relationship stands and wants some type of affirmation. I'm skeptical and don't like the blind side question. I mean I'm happy that she would be closer, but also very unsure of where we are going (or for how long we'll keep this going). I have had no intentions of dating anyone else at the moment, but she's adding pressure so I didn't seem to think it through completely.

The first thought that enters my mind is *"how could she just up and move along with her two small children to a new city after dating only six months?"* Granted she has 100 percent custody of the children, but she's thinking of removing the kids from their father who lives ten minutes away. Granted, she probably made a poor decision in marrying her ex-husband, but kids need to have their father in their lives. Another thing that really does not make sense is how incredibly impulsive and easy she is when considering this huge decision. We had only been in a "committed" relationship for a few months and she is willing to move her entire life. There had been no talk of our future, let alone an engagement (which certainly I would not even entertain). It seemed like a ridiculously spontaneous decision that immediately pressured me; I was being manipulated to fast-forward the relationship. I wasn't ready for that.

I had no idea at the time that impulsivity is one of the nine characteristics of a BPD, but this choice of leaving everything behind and moving her family was one of the first of many that met these criteria. Also, the deceitful way she used a job relocation as an excuse to move to Kansas City still leaves me scratching my head. As I reflect now, this was the first time that I saw how Jessica would do whatever it took to get what she wanted.

Not enthused about her idea nor totally opposed, I told her she should do whatever thinks is best for her and the kids. Within one week, she told me that she was looking online for jobs in Kansas City. I hesitated for a moment before asking what happened to her company's expansion office. Now I was given the answer that she isn't sure when it will take place, so she was looking for another job. I then realized this has nothing to do with a new job, but rather she was just looking for excuses to move to the same town as me.

She lines up several interviews in the next couple of weeks and is hired relatively quickly. I recognized that she was one extremely driven lady who is not going to stop, but only applied the thought to her career. She even pulled someone from her current office to move with her since that woman's boyfriend had been transferred to Kansas City - and they show up looking for apartments. She is very persistent and convincing, not necessarily completely a bad quality if you use it in your career. But when you take this characteristic into a friendship or relationship, it can generate resentment and form a lack of trust. I am sure she did a wonderful job of selling the move to her friend, because it met her own needs of a little bit more breathing room on expenses; they settled on an apartment ten miles from where I lived.

In just one month from her first thought about moving, Jessica was ready to move to Kansas City. I flew to Chicago to help her. In the eleventh hour, her associate had a change of heart and decides to stay in Chicago. Jessica doesn't bat an eye at the news and continues to pack. Her coworker is never heard from again and Jessica makes no effort to stay in communication, which I found completely strange. Mike, one of her closest friends whom I had met on several occasions, and I load the U-Haul; Jessica, her two kids and I then make the journey for KC. I find it ironic that the move is not because of her company expanding into the Kansas City area, but rather her intense desire to find a job in a world that has no real commitment from me. (In hindsight, I did discover six months later that there was never an expansion planned by her employer into the Kansas City area.)

So Jessica is now officially a resident of Kansas City. During the next several months, everything goes well; the kids get enrolled for the upcoming school year and we spend most of our time together. Jessica's total idealization of me and her tigress sex is still on full throttle, giving me positive feelings about the direction of our relationship right until another obstacle is thrown at me. By the end of the summer, Jessica informs me that her mother has lost her job in Illinois and wants to move down and live with them. It was concerning on how this would impact our relationship because from what I had seen, mother and daughter argued all the time. Both had

29

little, if any, respect for each other and it was disturbing as well as uncomfortable. Having such wonderful parents, I struggled getting my arms around any of their altercations. I had Dora sized up, and in addition to her being annoying, I speculated that there might be a change in Jessica's anxiety and personality that would filter down to me.

And I was right.

Chapter 4

Lying, Thieving…

It wasn't until September of 2003 that I ran into a major issue with Jessica's character. I received a call from her because she had been let go from her job, though she didn't seem very upset. She had been in the same field for ten years and felt now would be a good time to change to the pharmaceutical field. I encouraged her and told her I think that is a good decision. The job hunt goes slower than anticipated (not the least of which is because Kansas City isn't the heart of that industry), but I continue to be upbeat by telling her everything will be fine. Over the next two months, I tolerate her mother's snide and arrogant attitude, spending time with Jessica and the four children without Dora whenever possible.

In the early part of October, my ex-father in-law passes away and I make a trip to Southern Illinois with Jeremy and Aspen for the funeral. The morning before leaving, I noticed that my credit card balance was increasing, which seemed odd since I had been paying it off. I dropped by the bank to ask for the last four months of statements since I could not figure out why my balance was not decreasing. After looking at the statements, my mind and heart are racing because I can't think straight. There are charges from places where I have never shopped all over the statements — I discover over 70 transactions in the past 10 weeks totally $6500 that are unrecognizable.

And then my mind goes to Jessica. A few weeks prior, I was unable to locate my credit card in my wallet. She asked if

I looked in the night stand (yes) then suggested I look in the car in case it fell out. I ran to garage and start combing through the car when Jessica yells to me that she found it in the top drawer of the night stand, and gently accuses me of not looking closely. Again, I didn't see this issue for the bright sign it was until later in our relationship, because I wanted to believe that she could not have been so conniving 70 times. I try to cool off, but I am furious. My heart says there is no way but my mind has the evidence. Because I was leaving town for the funeral and pressed for time, I couldn't confront her right then in person. I called her cell phone. When she answered, I told her that I have found around 70 transactions on my credit card I did not make that add up to $6500 and asked if she knew anything about it. She replies in a very defensive tone that she absolutely had no idea what I was saying and even countered (to put doubt in my mind) by reminding me that I always have my credit card in my wallet, then challenged me with how could she do that when I always have my card.

I spent the next 30 minutes accusing her of taking my card and using it without my permission. Every time I tell her I don't believe her excuses, she denies the allegation and gives me some new reason she could never do such a thing. Her tactics actually start to work and I think to myself that I have to be wrong, no one would put up this much resistance and be so convincing if they were not innocent. It actually got me to wonder who used my card before I had to tell myself to stop thinking that way because the transactions are exactly where she shops. I know she did it! It is not until after an exhausting 45 minutes of talking to her that she finally confesses to the wrong doings. Yes, she took my credit card. Now I am confused and have no idea what to think. If she totally cares for me, why would she do this? Even after the confession, I am extremely bothered at her next statement: it was not her

32

fault she stole the but mine, because she was out of work and I should have offered to help pay for her expenses.

I have been driving close to an hour on the highway with the kids asleep in the car, and instead of wondering how I got to wherever the hell I am (both literally and proverbially), I can only think, "Holy Shit." I am being blamed for *her* stealing *my* credit cards. I admitted to myself that I had wondered sometimes about how she was paying her rent, utilities or when we might take the kids to do something, but thought the bills were being covered from her unemployment, Joe's child support payments and Dora's contributions. Her lying and theft were no match for the skill she had in turning the situation around to where it is my fault, actually nearly believing that I am part of the problem with her act of stealing.

Blaming another person or outside event is a common characteristic with highly functional borderline people. The BDP has a very difficult time in accepting accountability and they are hypersensitive for both actions as well as decisions. Jessica is no exception in this situation; instead of taking responsibility for not having a job and running low on money, *I* am the reason *she* is in her situation. She can't see herself as the source of her own financial burden because that would require her to feel guilt and shame; it may even remind her of the pain in previous childhood events. She portrays herself now as the victim and in her eyes, I am the bad guy. So many BPDs struggle to take responsibility for their actions because it will require them to look inside themselves, which generally does not happen without therapy. As I reflect to that first nine months of dating, there were many times when she would point out that I was the reason why something went wrong. Her comments were always direct, blunt and without any filter. During the early part of the relationship I did my best to treat this verbal Cuisinart as insignificant jabs, as I had no understanding of the cause of her sudden periodical accusations and outbursts. I continued to mistakenly attribute her shitty childhood and her parents for these situations.

I'm certain that my upbringing leads me to give people the benefit of doubt and trust people more easily, not seeing how they can cause their own problems. It's likely the reason I was in that position, but I had enough wherewithal to distance myself from her (and her mother) for a couple of weeks to think through everything. This doesn't stop her, though. She is focusing her determination on me, calling me repeatedly everyday to constantly apologize and wanting to know the status of our relationship. Her fear of abandonment appears again, though I know absolutely nothing about the BDP symptoms as this time; she starts to manipulate me back into her favor. It would take a lot of effort as she would discover, because I am so upset that I find it difficult to even imagine myself with someone who deliberately lied and stole from me.

One trait about Jessica (and most who suffer from BPD) is that when she wanted something badly enough, nothing would stop her from getting it. I can definitely put her in that category now. Combine this with extreme impulsive needs for their focused desire and there is absolutely no way to stop them. It can be a craving for cars, shoes, clothing or even a companion. After the weeks of Jessica calling and begging for forgiveness (because, of course, I am the focus of her impulse) along with her agreeing to repay the debt, I am lulled into believing that it is a onetime occurrence. With her not having a job and limited financial support, she has no other alternative but to file for another bankruptcy.

The next few months goes by relatively smoothly except for the increased amount of arguments about the most frivolous stuff, generally when we go out and alcohol is consumed or she has increased anxiety from her mother. I remember driving back from a party one evening when I turned to Jessica, and said, "I have argued with you more in one year than I did with my ex-wife in 14 years." I absolutely hate arguing and always have; I would start stonewalling, my preferred avoidance method, because I was tired of feuding all of the time. Silence would cause her increase her attacks — if you took one step back, she would take two steps forward. If I would ask her why you were arguing, she would say, "We are not arguing, we are discussing." Growing up, I would see my parents occasionally quarrel, but it was very limited. Jessica only saw bickering in her adolescence all the time from George and Dora. She had no skills for discussing sensitive matters in non-threatening way.

I found it hard to understand how someone could argue so much, and just attributed it to her natural tendencies. I can handle problems should they arise, but it seemed Jessica wanted to find or create issues every day — we could not go three or four days where there was not some form of "discussion." She was constantly starting arguments with me while also the new development of "blaming" me. Unfortunately, I gradually started to fall into the trap of arguing back. But I had the nagging feeling that I may be too deeply invested and maybe unable get out. When I realized her behavior was changing me, I told that her I thought it would be best we no longer see each other. It lasted a week before I reconsidered because I was not ready to leave the wonderful feeling of being idealized and good sex. Damn! Missed my chance at a clean escape.

Then there's another bump in the road about six months later when Jessica discovers she is pregnant. She seems to want to have the child, but silently I am completely opposed. I am still unsure about her and certainly don't want a child with her at this point in my life. I do everything tactfully as possible to talk her out of having the baby in spite of my Christian upbringing. I am able to convince of her that an abortion is the best choice for us and in the next few weeks, I go with her when she has the procedure. Jessica blames me many times for not wanting to have child, but I felt strongly enough about this decision and argument that we could not bring a child into the world. I later discovered that women suffering from BDP frequently get pregnant in order to entrap their mate into marriage or a deeper committed relationship. I'm so glad I made the right decision at that point.

Over the next several weeks, Jessica would mention how she wished we would have kept the baby, saying how cute it would have been and she was so sad at our decision. I did my best to sympathize with her because I knew this was a very difficult time for her, but when her moments of impulsive uncontrollable bitching would arise, all I could think was that I dodged a bullet.

Since pregnancy didn't work, within a couple months of the abortion she started to bring up the "M" word... yes, marriage. By then, I clearly saw her inconsistent behavior including episodes of major mood swings, blaming and frequent arguing. For Jessica, the best defense was a strong offense. I found it amazing how differently she could view the current world. If I (or anyone else) had a different way of thinking or beliefs, she would gladly correct me (or them) in a less-than-tactful way. I had experiences where she would pick fights and arguments with people out of the blue. It took very little to ignite her short fuse. These episodes did not happen consistently, but when they did... watch out. She blew up at one of my friends for no reason, just feeling like she needed to set him in his place. There was no need to attack him verbally, but it made me realize that I felt like a lion tamer trying to keep an animal under control, with no comprehension of her absolute way of thinking. I would come to learn this is called "splitting" in BPD.

Splitting is where BPDs see a person as either all good or all bad. There are NO shades of grey. You are either the king of the world or a piece of shit. BPD individuals consider if a decision is going to personally benefit them. If it does, they idealize and idolize those whom they feel have actions, wants and needs in parallel with their world. On the other hand, they can experience devaluation, which is exactly the opposite. The BPD person will dehumanize, criticize or disrespect you as quickly as you were put up on the pedestal. With splitting, the BPD often has a hard time developing any type of deep relationship since you seldom know where you stand and they frequently change their mind for no rational reason.

With Jessica, I started to notice that her idealization and devaluation is not always done directly face to face at people, but also she has this all-good-all-bad feeling towards people, actions and opinions even if she may not have contact with or know them at all. When she couldn't figure out how I felt about marriage, her tactics changed again and in the summer of 2004, she started pushing for us to move in together. She simultaneously focused on developing closer relationships with my children, especially Aspen.

I was still trying to sort out whether I can live with *her* for the rest of my life — I knew her mother would be part of the move, too, regardless of what the alternatives would be as her M.O. was so much like her daughter's. Living with Jessica would compound the burden of potential marriage, her mother always being a stone's throw away, and I was thinking about the how the kids would be affected (something that she didn't do - not in the move to Kansas City or later - because she saw children as pawns). As I look back now, I am shocked at how much effort she used with the children to take our relationship to the next level (but it was a sign so I really shouldn't be surprised).

Jessica reluctantly searched for apartments over the next month, displaying her displeasure that we aren't sharing my house. She is also disturbed that Dora will be still living with her and her boys. There was the theory that Dora would be forced to either get an apartment (which she could not afford) or move back to the condo in Europe that she inherited if Jessica lived with me. As the time for Jessica to move into a new apartment was just two weeks away, I began to second guess myself, relenting that she and the boys could move into my house. Somehow, Dora had no other option but to be forced to move into a hotel momentarily, exacerbating Jessica's pre-existing anxiety and Dora's bitterness towards Jessica. I remember thinking how she could be so heartless towards her mother, but it fit the mold of getting what she wanted. Part of me feels like I played a role in all the chaos and felt a little sorry for Dora, yet I had seen her negativity and condescending attitude so concrete that I realized Dora had made her bed and it was time to lay in it.

Jessica was delighted when I finally asked her to move into my house. I still had second thoughts although was happy with the idea of potentially putting together a family once again. Even though my beliefs went against two unwed parents with children moving into together (just as it had been opposed to abortion), I went against my core values, accepting it as a challenge while ignoring her erratic mood swings. The first six months went well as I did my best to deal with the drama, ignoring her complaining about unimportant issues. I compromised for peace and got to the point where I felt that this was just the way it was going to be, but soon Jessica had her eye on the marriage prize again and grew relentless day and night.

She cannot - is incapable - see my perspective, that a second marriage must work. She spends an enormous amount of time making me feel like I am the only one for her because her focus is all that matters. Over the next eighteen months, I find myself continually waffling about what I want. There are so many red flags I ignored, including my past experiences and lessons in therapy. For instance, while she has no respectful relationship with her parents, it doesn't matter because I am usually treated like the king of the castle. Looking back now, I feel she would have done anything to suck me into to her web, but it worked to her advantage because it felt so good to be on the pedestal.

She fed my focus on "family," knowing I wanted to repair my damage and pain from my first divorce. She reveled in our pseudo-family adventures, replacing her bleak childhood memories, and for her it just reinforced her desire for marriage. Simultaneously, the traveling, activities and living situation gave me a false sense of a "family unit" that I'd ignore the pains that came with the idealization of quasi-married life. Instead of asking myself if this was the right decision for me and the kids, I chose to continue drink the Kool-Aid of my youth... a husband, wife and children under one roof. But the way I was handling it — letting Jessica, Ian and Jake move in the house before we had a commitment — my parents and other relatives did not approve, even going so far as to have an aunt and uncle write a letter sharing that essentially I would burn in hell for living in the home unmarried. I didn't care what other people thought because I was stolen into a dream of my own life having a "family" again through her actions.

Chapter 5

The Manipulation

I approached 2005 with both apprehension and hope for where Jessica and I would be traveling down the road of courtship. Family vacations have occurred along with Christmas photo cards mailed; pictures of everyone are littered through the house. The children grow inch by inch and I make dinner every night for the "whole gang." I love the vision of four children sitting around the table, even as a couple of them are upset with the fact that they must eat their carrots. Since they are so close in age, they often banter as well as laugh back and forth about the daily scuttlebutt. There is nothing better than listening to young children talk about daily events from school and activities.

Since I only have my children half of the time, I spend a lot of my time with Ian and Jake while Jeremy and Aspen are with their mother. I find myself getting closer to them and treating them as my own flesh and blood. Their father is not a positive role model and rarely spoke to them; it is important for me to show them structure, provide a sense of family and (most importantly) be a father figure. Ian and Jake had moved a long distance into a new environment at such a young age, and I know that they need to see what a quality family setting means. My innate sense of providing a nurturing environment from my upbringing takes over most all other decisions, and I will make sure I do not let Ian and Jake down.

Jessica took a new job with a pharmaceutical company and seemed to enjoy her position. Dora was left with no other option than to move back to Europe and stay in her inherited condo for financial reasons. With the absence of Dora along with Jessica happy in her knew career, the flares in her moodiness seemed to level off. I find it a great relief and don't feel like I have to walk on eggshells all the time.

If I could pick one year to find a silver lining, it would be in 2005. There are only a handful of times during that year when Jessica lost her composure, only happening when she and I get into a fight (which would lead me to leave and chill out for a while). While we fought, there were times when she would barricade the door and tell me that I could not leave. Of course the more she said it, the more I felt the need to get out of the house. After making my way graciously through the human wall and getting into my car, she would call me repeatedly - sometimes 15 to 20 times - until I would answer. I could never understand why she was so damn persistent. Just let me have some distance for a while and I would be back with a clear head. I now know that she saw me leaving much more differently than me needing space. To Jessica, she saw me as abandoning her instead of considering my perspective. Her fears of abandonment from her parents were resurrected every time I would choose to flee the scene.

During that year, we spent our time doing all the things families do. The boys were enrolled into cub scouts, assisted at school events and spent quality time with everyone together. As the year wound down, we made plans to take the kids to Mexico for a family vacation. It was a wonderful time and I enjoyed watching the kids interact with the locals. Jessica and I had not fought for a while and she had not been criticizing or had any flip-out episodes for some time.

Yet, there are times where I did feel like I was being manipulated, especially when she got on the marriage kick. When she talked of marriage, she would threaten with phrases like, "If you're not going to marry me then maybe I should just leave." I would frequently reply, "That is your choice." I had realized that with her moving into the house that this would eventually crescendo, but still had many questions about marriage being the right decision for me and my children even while Jessica was continuing to fill my needs, feed my appetite; the sex was as strong as ever. I loved the fact that I could have sex whenever I wanted it along with the way she made me feel. I usually felt respected, loved and a sensation of something I had never felt, which was slowly becoming a codependency on her affection.

Approaching a year of being under the same roof really allowed me to get a better idea of her dual personality and behaviors. I was falling in love with someone who is smart, outgoing and affectionate. The side I did not like was often impatient, sometimes demeaning, overcritical, exhibited mood swings and consistently had "no filter." There was also a side I didn't know where to categorize — the effects of her childhood on her as well as our relationship. There were many signs that left me to question if I should continue down this road we had started, but my addiction to what we have built kept me in the game. I hoped that I was doing the right thing for the sake of me and the kids.

With winter approaching, I had my entire family over for the holidays. Jessica enjoyed entertaining, both preparing the feast and spending time with the family. She did a wonderful job at getting "in tight" with my family, but knew it was showtime since we were all under one roof. She was especially fond of my father and enjoyed bantering with him.

Over the several months before the holidays, she had made an enormous effort by calling and getting my father's opinion on things as well dropping by their house just to say hi. As I look back, I feel that she was laying the ground work for the approval of her with my parents. My dad definitely enjoyed her company and I was convinced had good feelings about her. Mom (being more soft spoken) never really said much, though she may have struggled with Jessica's outspokenness. Since Mom was extremely non-judgmental and understands it takes all types of people to make the world go round, I will never know how she felt about Jessica in the beginning.

New Year's Eve 2005 arrived and we spent time with the family at home watching the Times Square events. The kids were excited that they got to have sparkling cider as the clock counted down to midnight. They barely made it to 12:30 and were quickly rushed to bed. Jessica and I were tired as well and called it a night. I remember thinking what would be in store for 2006?

What it brought was Jessica's full court press to get married. Her bitching, criticizing and mood swings had seemed to disappear, which got us to the point where we started to talk about rings. I am a fairly frugal person and absolutely hate debt whereas Jessica tended to spend every dime she had (and mine, too), which caused her to file for bankruptcy twice already. I knew that she had a sizeable "rock" in her previous marriage (mainly from his sports betting earnings), and was unsure how we should handle the purchase of a ring. I happen to be an ebay freak and she decided that she would be content with an online purchase. I had been trying to pay off credit card debt and she knew that I would probably not want to spend more than $2500 since we would have to end up putting it right back on the credit card.

Even though she would not say it, she had been raised believing that cost of a gift (or in this case, a ring) was directly correlated to how much someone cared for you though I felt that it was more about the commitment two people have that makes the relationship.

In the middle of January, I made reservations for Valentine's Day, intending to propose over dinner. I racked my brain thinking of what I could do that would make this a unique and surprise occasion. With two days before the big day, I came up with the idea of making a special menu with creative dishes, wine, dessert and a picture of the ring on the final page. I happened to know the owner of the quaint Italian bistro where I had made reservations and let him know about my plan. He had been kind enough to lend me one of their menus and would let our waiter know about my plans. I had chosen not to get the ring in advance because I wanted Jessica to be able to pick out the size and style she wanted (and also because I had waited too long to order it online).

I was very excited and could hardly wait for dinner. She could tell I was acting differently and asked me what's wrong, with my reply being everything was just fine. We started off with a bottle of Merlot and talked about us and the children. Shortly after the first glass of wine, the waiter showed up and laid out the appropriate menus that I had designed. Jessica did not look at the menu for several minutes and I finally suggested that she might want to take a look at specials they were serving tonight. After what seemed like hours, she opened the menu and looked puzzled. Finally, after helping guide her through the entire menu, she looked up, smiled and screamed. I looked at her and popped the question; without a second thought, she answered yes!

She could not wait to begin looking for the style of ring she wanted. We revisited all of the sites from a few months earlier and she decided on the ring. I knew deep inside that she would struggle with the size of diamond that we had agreed upon, even though it was 2.02 carats. I felt it was pushing the grey area of being gaudy, but I thought she was happy and it was within our budget. Plus, I knew that size of the stone would make her feel important as well as impress her friends and coworkers.

Within a few days, the ring had arrived and she was ecstatic. Of course, people were impressed by the size of the ring. We spent the next several weeks letting everyone know about the engagement and showing off Jessica's new "rock." All of our friends were very happy to hear about the news. I found the next few weeks to be quite pleasant, with few outbursts or confrontations from Jessica. She was so perceptive to my "needs" during this time and would caterer to all of my wants. As always, it felt so great!

Approximately three weeks later, I was reviewing our credit card bill online and I saw an additional $550. Now, as part of the engagement, I had opened a new credit card with her as an authorized user to help build her credit from her bankruptcies, but she had agreed not to use it for anything else. I was caught off guard and came home to see if Jessica knew anything about the transaction. Of course, she said she didn't but right before I called the credit card company directly, she told me that she had decided to exchange her ring for a larger 2.5 carat stone. I could not believe what she was telling me. She was sending back a ring that we had both selected for a larger stone. She decided behind my back that out selection wasn't large enough and she needed a bigger ring. I was shocked at her deceitfulness, her decision to not discuss it with me and her shallow actions. I wasn't sure if I was more upset that she did not talk with me about the decision or if the fact that she felt like she needed something more than what I considered to already be a very large ring. I explained to her my disappointment that she wasn't accepting the ring I gave her; she agreed to call the company and not exchange the ring. Reflecting back, I think Jessica saw her identity through the size of her ring, boosting her image on how people would admire and perceive her.

Within a month, Jessica began talking about when we should get married. I really didn't feel the need immediately, but she wanted to do it sooner than later. She kept pushing for an October wedding (it was only March) and after hearing her constantly bringing it up every day, I agreed. By now, I had learned that Jessica was not the type of person that would take "no" for an answer because she would push and push until you gave in.

During the next six months, I started seeing a lot of Jessica's characteristics that were exactly like Dora's. Her constant arguing, bitching, impetuousness and disparaging actions left me questioning if I was making the right decision. Though not proud, I had coined a name for her ungratified bitchy moods by calling her "Doressica" when her ugly side popped out. I knew how much she despised her mother, so in a way I was hoping that she would recognize how she was acting like Dora, thus open her eyes and stop. Unfortunately, the moniker sent Jessica into the next level of impulsive hysteria actions and verbal jabs. Hindsight is 20/20, and I should have never said the moniker as most people do not want to be compared to their parents (which held true for Jessica). However, at drawing attention to the similarities, it made her dislike the person she saw inside much more. I am sorry.

Summer approached and Jessica was engulfed in her new focus - the details of the wedding. She thought it would be nice to have my father preside over the wedding (he is an ordinated minister). We asked, and he was happy to oversee the service. There were other details we needed to discuss, such as expenses. It's typically the wife's family that pays for the ceremony (which meant the two of us would be paying), so I was hoping since this was our second marriage we could try and keep to some type of budget while still making it a special day. We needed to pick a church, then decided we wanted something a little more casual, but somehow a week later she had decided we'd marry at the local country club. Whereas I thought we could look into it, she did more than check it out. She had signed us up as members, which also meant we would have to pay dues as well as buy all the food, beverages, cake and alcohol from them.

She was in her focused "no other opinion" mode. We didn't talk about it because she had decided it was a good deal. She didn't ask about prices, and tried to explain it away as a social membership "only $90 a month and we have to spend at least $300 a month on food and drink, but we get to use the pool." Her impetuous decision to obligate us to more debt and the obligation of at least $390 a month for the next two years was mind boggling! On top of that expense, we still had to pay for all the food and drinks for the entire wedding. This "good deal" of hers was not looking so great. Basic math: $20 dollars a person for food times 100 guests with an $2500 in drinks along with $500 for the country club's cake and the $9360 in membership dues for the next two years. I did my best of biting my lip about her making decision of joining the country club, but again encouraged her to talk with me before making a commitment or large purchases. As usual, she apologized and I told her it was okay. It was a powerful reminder that Jessica always does and gets what she wants.

Her next focus was looking for her dress. Without more insight shared with me on the dress, she then headed to a florist and comes back that night, saying she can get what she wants for $250, which seemed reasonable. I am not sure why a bouquet costs that much, but let it go. Her wheels were in motion; I was ready to commit my life to Jessica. We were able to enjoy the summer with the majority of the time spent at our new country club pool. Jessica enjoyed laying out at the pool while the kids swam. It was probably the major reason why she chose it as the facility for the wedding. The summer flew and we found ourselves getting the children ready to start school as well as finalizing the invitation list. Quite frankly, her temperament had been great the last four months after the fight about the country club and I found it delightful to be with her.

She didn't invite her parents as Dora had moved back to Greece (and was unable but most likely unwilling to make it back) while George hadn't spoken to her in close to 13 years. With no one to walk her down the aisle, she asked her good friend, Mike, if he would come in from Chicago to do the honors; he gladly accepted. We had chosen not to have any bridesmaids or groomsmen - only our children. On the wedding day, everything looked perfect! With a full house, I took my cue from my father and walked down the aisle; then the boys walked together and finally Aspen appeared as the flower girl. The music began and our guests rose to admire the bride. Slowly, Jessica and Mike walked down the aisle as several tears rolled down my cheek when I saw how stunning she looked. My dad calmly cleared his voice and stated, "Who gives this bride?" Mike looked to Jessica and gave her a hug before answering, "I do."

Dad delivered a touching and inspiring message. We said our vows, did the big kiss and then the celebration started. Everyone lined the bar or food line while the DJ started to play his tunes. It was great to see all of our friends gathered and celebrating the next step of our journey. The night was amazing and went almost drama free. I say almost because my aunt and uncle (the ones who wrote us the letter stating how they disapproved of the situation) attended, thus giving Jessica energy that it was her right to give them a piece of her mind and to admonish them. I begged her not to confront them, that it would only create an uncomfortable feeling among the family. To my amazement, this was one of the few times she bit her tongue and did not make a scene.

Her seduction had worked and I was now a sucker in the relationship.

Chapter 6

Her New Weapons

With the wedding behind us, we were able settle into a normal family routine. Like little soldiers, the kids marched out the door every morning to where the bus picked them up in front of our house. All three boys were active at that point in karate two week nights and Saturdays. We enrolled the boys in Cub Scouts and Aspen in Brownies. We had our first Thanksgiving together as a unified family the month following the wedding and had the entire extended family over to celebrate. For the first time since my divorce, I felt like I had my family back and I felt complete.

It wasn't long before I made a mistake and would never hear the end it from Jessica. The first week of December in 2006, we attended the children's Christmas program at school — both Ian and Jeremy performed. After the program ended, Jessica asked me if I could get Jake from Cub Scouts, to which I agreed. Since I had more than an hour and half before his scouting event was over, I told her I was going to swing by a restaurant (with one more meal that quarter). She asked me not to stop, but I told her I had a lot of time to kill and walked out the school.

Being close to Christmas, the place was pretty busy. I had a beer; I looked at my watch and saw I still had 40 minutes before picking up Jake, so I ordered another. I saw some friends and spent time talking before wishing them all a good holiday and headed to my car. I left the parking lot to get

Jake and could not have been a couple hundred feet from the restaurant when a police car was following me. The siren turned on and I pulled over. He approached the car and I rolled down the window. The officer asked if I knew why I had been pulled over, and I replied, "No, sir." He stated that my tires had touched the outside lines of the road and then proceeded to ask me if I had been drinking. I answered, "Sir, I had two beers back at the restaurant," and showed him the receipt showing a total of $8.33 including tip. He didn't care about the receipt and asked me to get out of the car and stand in front of the police car, where I was asked to perform several sobriety tests. He also wanted me to take a breathalyzer. Having several attorney friends, they had always advised not "to blow" if you were to get pulled over — I was put into the back of his car and taken to the police station.

I was asked again if I would like to blow, to which I again replied no. I was escorted into a holding area and told that I could use the phone. I remember thinking about Jessica's reaction as I dialed, especially as it was ten minutes past the time I was supposed to get Jake. She answered the phone and just like I expected, I got an ear full like a mother scolding a child, causing me to resent her attitude. I let her know that I will need $500 for bail and that I would be waiting for her to arrive. About 30 minutes later, she showed up and I was released (though I wasn't sure if I wanted to stay in jail or hear her reprimand me all the way home). She berated me, told me that I reminded her of her ex-husband who had gotten three DUI's in 18 months; she complained of having to explain it to her mother, who recently moved back from Greece since she mom picked up Jake.

We had been married two months, and now when I look back, this was moment that tide began to change in the relationship. The idealization that she showed me over the four years while dating was changing into devaluation. She would chastise me over insignificant things, such as why I picked up chicken instead of ground beef at the store. These encounters would turn into an all-out attack of my intelligence and character. I was routinely left feeling like a "bad little boy" being scorned by his mother.

It was also about the time when she persuaded a doctor with whom she worked to write her a prescription for phentermine, a proven appetite suppressant similar to Phen-Fen that she believed was going to be her answer for putting on a few extra pounds. Almost immediately I noticed an increase in Jessica's intensity. She was already one of the strongest willed, impatient and hyper people I knew; now with this amphetamine, her character ascended to a whole new level. Just when I thought there was no way she could be any more high-strung than she already was, out came the little white pill that I started calling Phenter-MEAN!

Three months after getting married, we started 2007 with her employer getting acquired by another pharmaceutical company, so she would have to go out of town several weeks for training in Las Vegas. Though more demanding on me handling everything for the kids, I noticed that the house was much calmer. Her intense boisterous voice was absent and the five of us felt like we were not constantly monitored. I missed her, yet I found it kind of nice not being on pins and needles.

A few days before she was scheduled to return home, she called to talk to all of us. After talking to me for a few minutes, she had me try to guess what she had done. Dread filled me as I waited for the answer; she had gotten a tattoo. I was floored since we both had talked about how we really didn't care for body art, yet she displayed this high degree of spontaneity while out of town for work. Throughout our relationship I thought her sense of adventure was fun and attractive, but this reversal of opinion after voicing such negative beliefs just weeks earlier was excessive. I was a little bothered, but it just got stored as another "red flag."

Once she returned from training, we argued more than ever. I reverted to my stonewalling tactic, but now she would demean me to get a response. If that did not work, she would hit lower until she could finally push one of my buttons (which she managed to do every time she picked a fight in front of the children). I absolutely despise arguing in front of kids, or anyone for that matter. If there is a problem, take it behind closed doors. For Jessica, it's in her DNA to fight anywhere.

One night, she claimed I was a cheap person when it came to dining out, picking the fight while the children were in the back seat. With six mouths to feed and her preference for going out to eat, it started to add up; yes, I would at times have the kids split adult sized meals. That evening, we both had cocktails with our meals, though I knew alcohol was a slippery slope for her — it would make her interrupt while responding because it freed her to say what she wanted and disregard anyone else's thoughts more than usual. We left the restaurant and started for home. While she cranked it up with more belittling of me and my frugalness, I could only focus on how it's not good in front of the kids. I finally reached across inconspicuously give her a little pinch on her leg to get her attention and ask her to please stop. Instantly, she gets the kids involved, getting me to react just like she wanted.

In the past there had been times where she mischievously belittled me in front of the kids when I would play it off, but this time was different. It was continuous digs and she was doing it in front of all the children with her leading them to side with her point of view. She continued her manipulation of the past but in new ways — using the kids. I tried to avoid more of her behavior by going to bed. The next morning, she asks if I want to have sex. When I tried to bring up being bothered at her behavior the night prior, she returns to calling me cheap, and then apologizes so she can get sex because it's increasingly only about what she wants.

Over the next month, I do my best to forget the altercation in front of the kids and try to file it as one of those speed bumps that occur in a marriage; however, the arguing between us increases, even more than in the past. The attacks and blaming towards me are getting old, but I do my best to turn the other cheek because I am focused on my need for a happy family life.

Five months into our marriage and I see a side of her that sticks out to this day. In March, I was invited to my best friend's birthday party and we both attended. One of Jessica's friends, Robyn, decided to come, too, so we decided to just drive together. It was good to see a lot of fellas I had not seen in some time. The evening was going well, but as the night progressed Jessica was getting into one of her intense belligerent moods (which normally goes hand-in-hand with how much she has to drink). I had learned that when she gets like that, I had to walk a very tight rope. She generally tends to be very direct, rambunctious, loud and playfully combative with anyone around her. All of the gates to the dam are wide open and there are no restrictions to her action or what might come out of her mouth. NONE! The best thing to do when she enters into this mood is to stay very far away from her and *definitely* do not get on her bad side.

The party shifted from the restaurant to one of Kansas City's trendy night life areas. We spent the rest of the evening drinking and celebrating my friend's birthday. Jessica, right along with Robyn, continued to drink steadily and I continue to watch her mood crescendo. I was starting to get tired around midnight, so I suggested we should leave for home. I knew there might be a chance of her balking at the idea, but surprisingly she agreed. The three of us left the bar and started to walk towards the valet when we saw a larger crowd of people including, unexpectedly, a guy that Robyn had recently stopped dating and who happened to be out with another lady. I knew that he had just gotten out of prison for allegedly shooting one of his coworkers (the court was unable to prove it due to a technicality). Point being, this was one guy I knew that the ability to be a very mean, vindictive and I wanted nothing to do with him.

I tried divert the girls to the valet area so we could pick up the car and get the hell out of there. My plan worked momentarily until Robyn decided she needed to confront him. Almost immediately the two of them started having words; I was just hoping the car would show up soon. They continued to argue until the car arrived and Jessica had to literally manhandle Robyn into the car. With everyone in the car and me at the wheel, I start to pull away. Yet Jessica's bravado rolled down the window, so she could lean her head out and shouted, "Ben, how does it feel to be out of prison?" Instantly, I grabbed Jessica's arm firmly and tried pulling her back into the car. She continued shouting at Ben and finally on my third attempt, I was able to get her back into her seat. I couldn't believe she was taunting him, but it was what Jessica wanted, so she did it.

We pulled away and Jessica was irate with me. She started by calling me a fucking asshole. Though I tried to explain I didn't want there to be a confrontation with a man who had gone to trail for murder, she pulled Robyn as her witness. She taunted me by calling me a fucking jerk and doubted her reasons for marrying me. I decided to pull the car over in an empty lot and told her I was not going to drive any longer if she was going to act this way. I got in the back seat next to Robyn as she became even more hostile with her words, chastising at full throttle. I quietly took out my phone to record the what she was saying. One jab after another rolled off her tongue. She pushed me to get back and drive, then called me a fucking piece of shit when I again refused. She makes comments like I don't care about her job, I want her to be caught drinking and driving as well as blistering me with accusations of having short man's syndrome and that I am a fucking loser. This continues for close to 15 minutes before she hopped in the driver's seat and proceeded to drive home. I felt like I had been verbally raped.

At home, I headed straight to bed while Robyn continues to listen to Jessica. I cannot believe I married her. I awoke with her asleep next to me about 3 a.m. with my mind still racing about what had taken place. I quietly got dressed and grabbed my laptop, then headed up the road to an IHOP where I could get a cup of coffee and Wi-Fi. I login to my computer and Google the phrase "divorce in Missouri without using an attorney." I go through page after page of a bunch of legal jargon I really did not understand. I spent the next hour and half looking but got no clear cut answers, so I headed home in disbelief that I am thinking about this while only married for a little over five months.

For the next couple of days, we really didn't talk much with one another. When all the issues did come up, she wanted to blame me for pulling her too hard into the car while she ignored my explanation that Ben was the type of person who could hurt her and my actions were all for concern about her livelihood. Monday rolled around and I decided to drop by the court house to see if they had any information about getting a divorce without an attorney. They only suggested I go to one of the local college libraries to research it. On my drive home I thought of how much of an idiot I was, because who gets divorced after five months?

Later that week after my trip to the courthouse, Jessica can feel my distance and finally apologizes. She said she does not really remember most of what happened and asked if we can put this in the past. She started concentrating her attention and affection towards me over the next several months. I could not forget the situation. I found myself being less tolerant, becoming more defensive while using more stonewalling, which I know pushed her buttons. It was a high conflict relationship and she continued to manipulate to get what she wants, sometimes with sex and sometimes with arguments. I grew accustomed to her drama and her frequent tirades by telling myself that this is just the way my wife was wired. Somehow, I was still committed to the marriage and loved her dearly.

Chapter 7

Female Wars

Summer and fall of 2007 was a low drama period by previous standards. Sure, she would have sporadic breakouts from time to time, but I was able to manage them (for the most part). The children were back in school and involved again with activities. Ian and Jeremy were playing football and we decided to have Jake try his hand at wrestling. I wrestled in high school and was excited to see how he would do since he was extremely strong and fast for his size/age (with an orneriness about him that I felt would help him excel).

As winter approached, I started to notice a change in Aspen and Jessica's relationship. The once empathic and caring woman (now Aspen's stepmother) was much more critical of my daughter, causing Aspen to clearly struggle with the way she was being treated by Jessica. I am unsure why she was being so harsh toward Aspen and not the boys. While I'm not the type to play favorites among the children and did my best to treat all them equally, I knew that being the only girl among the four kids had to be difficult on Aspen. I should have spent a little more time with her when she was taking bullets of criticism from Jessica. So many times in a blended family, the biological parent tries to protect their own children, and I made sure I was not one of "those" parents. In fact, I hate to admit it, but I probably tried to spend more time and do extra things for both Jake and Ian since I knew they were missing a father figure.

I could not exactly put my finger on why Aspen was acting out the way she was; in addition to my marriage, my ex-wife had been dating someone for close to a year and had been married six months. That's a lot for a young girl to handle if not dealt with correctly. After noticing the differences and talking with my ex-wife, we felt it might be best for Aspen to go talk with a child therapist. The first few times, the therapist asked me to join Aspen in the office and discuss exactly why she was here. Then Aspen began going into the office alone. Jessica was always so inquisitive about what was discussed in Aspen's sessions. I found that to be a little odd; a patient/therapist relationship should be somewhat private unless the individual chooses to talk about those topics with other people.

On one particular week, both my ex-wife and I had a commitment and were unable to take Aspen to her appointment, so I asked Jessica if she could drive her and she eagerly accepted. That was rather strange because she was enthusiastically helping, but did not think much about it. About a week later, I received a call from the therapist asking me if I could come to Aspen's next visit. Upon arriving at the next session, the therapist called me into her office while Aspen sat in the lobby. She mentioned that Jessica seemed to think I had been drinking too much and secondly that she (Jessica) understood that Aspen had a problem with the gentleman my ex-wife had been dating. I asked if Aspen told her these things and she said no, that Jessica brought it up in the last session. The therapist just wanted me to be aware of what was discussed and ask if I would send Aspen in for their meeting.

As I waited in the lobby for the visit to finish, all I could think about was Jessica's latest maneuver. First, she went into my daughter's therapy session. I was surprised that the therapist allowed Jessica into the private session as they had been private for several weeks. The fact that Jessica brought up these issues and not Aspen made me feel like I was being manipulated. Next, she complained about things we've never had surface as a problem. Yes, I did come home from the gym and enjoy having a few glasses of wine while I prepare dinner for everyone. I had done this since the day they moved into the house. Cooking is my down time for the day. Then, I also realized that Jessica was making comments about my ex's new husband, which meant again, she was using the therapist as a pawn in her way to control me. All of this seemed malicious.

That evening, I approached Jessica about what she told the therapist. Her retort was that she didn't want me to drink at night. Jessica never brought up the conversation with me, so I asked her why she didn't talk to me with the added twist of why she brought up my ex's new husband. I had known the man for several years and felt like he was a great guy. She, of course, had a different opinion by stating that she had heard some things and didn't much care for him. What?! She didn't even know him! Continuing to fight, she replied saying that one lady at the country club said that he can be kind of flirty. I finished by saying these are issues that you have, not the feelings of Aspen, and that I did not appreciate her using the therapist as tool for her propaganda.

I was starting to learn that Jessica had a methodical way of manipulating certain situations where she had something to gain on me, friends or even the kids. More pandemonium follows that fall in September of 2007 when one of my good friends called and invited us to an 80's concert. The venue was packed and predominantly African American, though there were a few of us old school Caucasians that loved R&B throughout the crowd. We got our groove on and made some new friends around us. One couple behind us was an Asian gentleman and African American young lady. I am not exactly sure of their relationship, but one thing for certain was the promiscuous and forward comments the woman made towards me. I had hoped Jessica didn't hear since that would open up a very large can of worms. The band finished playing and we were invited back to a VIP area. I made my way through the appetizer line when I ran into the young lady and she decided to help herself to one of the hors d'oeuvres on my plate. Jessica was several people behind me and did not see her help herself, however someone else did and made sure she knew.

Jessica immediately approached the lady and asked her what she was doing. The lady made a fairly smug remark and before I knew what happened, Jessica pushed her several times like a rag doll and it made her wig fly off. I was in total dismay until the woman's presumed boyfriend flies in from nowhere and put me in a headlock. I can't figure out why he is starting a fight with me; I didn't do anything! Jessica is the one who started the fight and now I am thrown into the middle of this skirmish. My drink's glass shattered into many pieces as we wrestled for several seconds. Security guards broke up the brawl. The altercation could not of been more than 10 seconds, but I managed to cut my hand as well as arm, so blood was everywhere.

We were escorted down to the security office where police officers questioned me about what happened. As I told the story, all that ran through my mind is *what the hell*! Jessica started this whole thing, and here I sit with blood all over my clothes being interrogated by the police. I had never been in a fight and now in my mid-40's, my wife can't control her anger. I am potentially going to be hauled off to jail because of her. The officer eventually asked if I wanted to press charges against the gentleman and I told him no. Jessica showed up in tears and apologized. I could not understand why she couldn't control her temper. The answer is simple that she cannot. She only knows how to defend her inner feelings and does not possess the ability of any rational decision making when she doesn't get what she wants. The more I thought about it, the more I started noticing that when Jessica drinks that there will be more verbal fights and physical conflicts. The change between an upbeat outgoing person into a mean castigating individual can happen in a split second, particularly when she has been drinking.

Things are calm for a month as the football season ends for Ian and Jeremy. We turn our attention to Jake and his new endeavor with wrestling. Not surprisingly, he takes to it like a fish to water and Jessica spends three evenings a week taking him to practice as well as getting to know the other parents. On the weekends, we all find ourselves sitting in gymnasiums all day watching hundreds of boys roll around on the mats in tournaments. The sport is very time consuming, but we both became very involved with his success. One thing that was very noticeable is the degree of intensity Jessica brings to each of the matches. She could be the extremely vocal and passionate mother that can be heard throughout the gym, but compounded by having a gym full of people's eyes and ears on her. She becomes the image of her father focused on her when she ran track. Certainly there is nothing wrong with supporting your child and being vocal; however, Jessica took it to the next level and it became obsessive. (Eventually, this wonderful sport would be one of major stumbling blocks to our marriage.)

We finished up the year like previous years with my extended family over for both Thanksgiving and Christmas, but best of all for me there is less than normal drama from Jessica during the holiday season. I was committed to our marriage, but Jessica's actions left me very confused our first year. There were so many high peaks and deep valleys in our relationship. We had been together for five years, but once the vows were said and she got the ring slipped on her finger, there definitely was a change in the relationship — and then Jessica was interested in breast implants. As the years went forward, it became more about the show than the substance.

The large amount of weight (some of which was engorgement with milk) while being pregnant caused her breasts to become very stretched. Afterwards, they became saggy with considerable stretch marks and returned to her original A cup. She was very self-conscience about how they looked and wanted to do something about it (though her self-consciousness never was an issue before our marriage or interfered with our crazy sex). I had absolutely no problem with the way she looked since I loved her for who she was (not how her breasts looked), but I understood why she was concerned. Typical of going for what she wanted and without any discussion with me, she consulted with a doctor. I was again bothered that she had made such an impulsive decision without even talking with me. I tried to compromise by suggesting that we take the next four months to save the $5500 for the procedure as I was still trying to pay off other bills from her credit card. I was upset when she told me she had already scheduled the operation in three weeks.

Though we fought about paying for it, she said her mother was going to pay from some money she had. This seemed to be stretching the truth, but I went along to keep the peace. A few weeks later, I opened up a letter from the doctor's office showing a copy of a check with Jessica's name on it from a different bank other than our joint account. I was confused because I was unaware of any other checking account that she had, so I asked her. She became defensive saying I should not have opened the envelope because it was from her doctor. I reminded her that I generally open all the mail, that the bigger problem was the copy of check that had her name as single account holder. She admitted she never told me about her bonuses at work so she paid for it with her own money. Own money! How did she not understand we were equals in the marriage and needed to be upfront about everything. Discussions included my bonuses — why not hers?

She has manipulated me again as well as lied to me. I am not bothered about her operation, but how she handled the matter. She impulsively decided to do whatever she wanted. Once again, if Jessica wanted something, she would get it no matter what the consequences.

Chapter 8

Wrestling, George and Promiscuity

With Jake's first season of wrestling behind us, Jessica inquired about a wrestling academy where only the best athletes in the region are invited to participate. She took Jake to several sessions and the coaches were seeing his potential. They eventually asked him to become part of the group. Jake was ecstatic and honored to be part of the academy. This decision not only comes with a huge time commitment, but also a heavy financial responsibility for the family's budget. I knew that it meant a lot to both Jessica and Jake, so I didn't object.

With a lot of enthusiasm, we would often find Jake with his gym bag packed and pressuring Jessica to hurry up so he would not be late to practice. Starting in the spring of 2008, just two years after we were married, his practice schedule consisted of Monday through Thursday evenings for three hours and then a full seven-hour session on Sundays. Needless to say, there are many nights where I am alone with one to three children waiting to get into bed until they arrive home.

The academy was a year-round responsibility located 45 minutes away, so there was no reason for Jessica to drive back home to just turn around and drive back to pick up Jake. After several months of attendance, she was meeting many of the wrestlers' parents and making new friends. As one might expect, most of the parents that attended are men, and with Jessica's outgoing personality and attractive looks, she was often invited out for drinks and dinner with the fathers while the boys practiced. Within six months, Jessica was considered one of the fellas and frequently received text and phone call from one particular father in the group. At first I did not think too much about it, but I mentioned to her that I thought it was a little odd how often he talked with her. Her response was defensive and ranged from rationale that he was just a friend to he wasn't attractive as well as he's married; it's not her fault that the man liked her because she was outgoing, fun and attractive.

I did my best to overlook the ongoing attention from the man, but in the back of my mind I felt Jessica was not taking a firm enough stand in distancing herself from his suggestive behavior. I felt that she was giving mixed signals - intentionally - even though they may be small. She took no accountability and constantly deflected "fault" to the father. I would have been appreciative if she admitted she was getting vibes that this man was hitting on her, if she distanced herself or told him there was no interest because she was committed to our marriage. Instead, she does nothing for six months and finally things come to a head.

In the summer of 2008, we were asked to go on a canoe float trip (just a family thing we do in the midwest) with many of the wrestler's parents. Adam, the man that talked to her all the time, ended up going, too. He brought his son though his wife stayed at home with their other children. After finishing dinner, everyone gathered around several campfires and the adult beverages began to flow. We spent several hours conversing while everyone continued to get liquored up. By 10 o'clock, I was ready to turn in and told Jessica I was going to hit the sack, but she told me she was going to stay up a while longer. I went back to the cabin and proceeded to fall asleep.

I woke up when she entered the room, and could see she was upset. I took the bait and asked why. Adam had stuck a beer bottle in her crouch as she had bent over to get a drink in the cooler. Hearing the news upset me for a couple of reasons, not only because this man thought he could touch my wife, but also she was giving an impression that she was tempting Adam.

This whole "Jessica flirting with other men" thing caused me to second guess myself if she had told the truth about the overtures all being Adam's fault, and I decided that she is flirtatious unconsciously. One other thing I noticed is that she has only a few female friends, and they are generally softer spoken, which allows Jessica to be the center of attention when she is around them. If there are more outspoken women, these friends are generally the ones where she has had confrontations (then excludes them until she needs something). I always found it rather odd how one day she would be a supportive friend only to distance and criticize them the next.

The incident blew over that night and we stayed away from Adam that weekend, but soon enough there was another reason for her to get fired up. George decided to reenter Jessica's life. Her phone rang and George's voice was on the end of the other line. They spent a fair amount of time talking and one thing Jessica discovered was that he had a heart attack several months ago. He started cycling to help his recovery. My guess was that it took a life threatening situation like the heart attack for George to have the epiphany of picking up the phone and calling his only child, to whom he had not spoken in 20 years.

They spent the next month communicating; Jake and Ian were allowed to finally converse with their grandfather. The boys seemed to enjoy talking with the mystical person called Grandpa who has been absent their entire life. Yet, the ability to connect with George appears to have both its pros and cons. The boys liked having a humorous, stern and overly opinionated missing piece of their extended family; however, they discover his dysfunctional side in just a couple of weeks.

It wasn't long before the boys started giving us summaries of the phone calls. Sadly, we found out that he talked badly about Jessica and Dora as well as used profanity. I didn't understand how he could degrade their mother without ever having met the boys and cursing around the children was such a strange choice. Jessica confronted George, but he was quick to validate his actions by making it clear that no one will tell him what to do. The phone calls continued anyway through the next month and I was confident he does not change his actions. The boys, however, learn it is better not to talk about their conversations. As the end of summer approaches, George talked to Jessica about the opportunity of meeting the boys and taking them for a week. She was perplexed about the idea of handing of the boys to someone they had never met even though it is their grandfather. After a few days thinking about it, she decided it might good for them to finally meet their grandpa. They picked a date and halfway point where they would meet. The children were excited, but Jessica continued to worry if she was making the right decision.

Jessica travelled four hours to make the transfer at the selected meeting place. As they pulled into the parking lot, she could see George waiting in his car. She was extremely nervous and even scared since she had not seen him in so long. He made his way to their car and everyone hopped out. George immediately greeted the boys with a hug and told them it was nice to finally meet them. He was cordial to Jessica but doesn't say "it's good to see you" or "I missed you." Instead, he blurted, "wow, it looks like your ass is getting big!" After so many years, George still carried the bitterness and lack of empathy towards his only child. I can't imagine how she felt at that moment. All she had ever wanted to feel since being a young girl is the sense of love and nurturing from her dad. His nastiness was just a reminder of disappointment of an entire lifetime.

She headed home full of anxiety and second guessing her decision to allow George to have full rein of the children for a week. It seemed to last forever since George would not let the boys call regularly and when they did, there was always something disturbing they would mention. It was almost like he was putting the boys through military basic training exercises: only letting them to eat limited food, prolific profanity and strict orders on how they should act and think. He even took them on an expedited trip to Tennessee so they could see where their great-grandfather was buried. After an eight hour journey, they spent five minutes at the grave and hopped right back in the car to return to George's house. Certainly the most disturbing thing he did (besides belittling Jessica and Dora) was telling the boys the story of when Jessica swallowed a bottle of aspirin and had to be rushed to the hospital to have her stomach pumped, which we discovered after they returned home.

The children finally arrived back home and both we got the summary of what took place over the week. We were told about all of George's structured behavior. With all of the recent incidents of Jessica's behavior and George's story uncovering the potential suicide attempt reminded me later that this should have been another red flag among the many others that I had started to see over the past several years. Jessica always did such a beautiful job of downplaying self-destructive behavior that after a few weeks I file incidents away and forget about them.

Even though both Jessica and I felt George was not the best influence on the boys, we still allowed George to continue to talk them occasionally. In early fall, she had been invited to a class reunion back in Illinois and mentioned to George we would be in town. I finally had the opportunity to meet the man. We entered the restaurant and there sat George in a pair of shorts and an Army sweatshirt. I found it odd that he was wearing shorts since it was about 40 degrees outside, but this was part of his persona. Let's face it, the clothing told part of the story: I am tough because I am not only wearing shorts, but I also am wearing Army gear. He might as well of had a shirt that had printed, "Don't fuck with me!"

We sat down and Jessica introduced me; I told him it was nice to meet him. Similar to Jessica in one of her moods, it became very clear to me to keep the peace, so I allow George to lead the conversation *and* agree with everything he had to say. Just as advertised, he was clearly one of the most opinionated and head-strong people I had ever met, yet he was extremely pleasant to the young lady that served us. He was definitely a regular customer and she talked very highly of him. While George used the men's room, she made a point to come over and mention how much he talked about his grandchildren. She also made a comment how most people don't really understand him and that "his bark is much louder than his bite." (I'm not sure the rest of the community would have agreed.) We finished our meal and George was kind enough to offer to pay the bill. I certainly was not going to put up any resistance and thanked him. He was polite to me, but I definitely saw a side to him that would emerge as a fierce unmerciful person and father... and push the buttons of my wife.

Chapter 9

My Buttons Are Pushed

In the latter months of 2008, we were fighting more than normal — criticizing, blaming and emotional jabs took place regularly. I had grown accustomed to her explosions, but now they were taking place several times a week. All too often I started thinking to myself, "I have to get out of this marriage." You could also see that it was having an adverse effect on the children. Jessica's relationship with Jeremy was in a downward spiral and it had gotten worse with Aspen; Jessica blamed the children as the problem.

Between the obsession with Jake's wresting, me spending my nights alone as Jessica was always at wrestling events (sharing the child's spotlight) and increased amounts of fighting, I felt less respected in the relationship. I continued to deal with countless amounts of lies, manipulation and deceit from Jessica. It was starting to wear on me and my character as a person. I hate arguing, but it was happening so often. This was actually the beginning of me not liking the person I was becoming; I started drinking more to numb myself from the unhappiness in the marriage. Jessica's emotions got more and more erratic as well as unpredictable.

We finished the year by taking a Christmas vacation back to an area in Mexico we had previously visited. I was hoping that she would be able to relax and reflect on some of the good times because I really needed to get some reprieve from her tempestuous behavior. I also needed to not be wary of her every action. I was actually surprised that Jessica agreed to take the vacation since it was right in the middle of wrestling season and typically she felt any time away from the sport might affect Jake's progress. Nevertheless, the time away with the family was very enjoyable, and with Jessica in a good mood the entire week, it reminded me of the early days of dating.

Regrettably, the tranquil drama free time was short lived. Almost on cue, when the plane returned to Kansas City so did her criticizing, blaming, intense mood changes and all the other negative characteristics. I didn't know how much longer I could continue to take verbal attacks and inconsistencies of not knowing whether I was going to get "Good" or "Bad" Jessica. I had always tried to be patient, but after doing my best to keep my composure and bite my tongue, I would fall short during 2009. My buttons had been bulldozed so many times in so many ways; I chose to start pushing back since stonewalling was no longer working. I love Jessica more than I have loved anyone, but I am beginning to identify the disparity between her words and her actions. My heart was battling with my better judgment, yet I continued to stay faithful towards making the marriage work.

In early February while watching the Superbowl that I had finally reached my boiling point. It was the first time of several instances where I was shameful of my actions. I am not going to try and justify myself, but I will say I was tired and beat down. During the game, Jessica attempted to start an argument and I did my best to not fall into the trap. So she proceeded to start picking on Aspen, and made horrible comments about her acting like a little bitch and continued to tee-off on my daughter. I stood up and went into our bedroom, knowing she would follow me still in a tirade. My mind was saying STOP, but the chastising kept going with no end in sight. I absolutely couldn't take it any longer and went over to her work printer, put my foot through the top and broke the glass. It is difficult for me to understand why I did what I did, but the only way to describe it like having a bully on the playground that keeps pushing and calling you names repeatedly until finally you lose composure and fight back. That night, she finally hit the right button.

Needless to say, after I destroyed her printer, she was enraged and began directly verbally assaulting me. I have nothing to say. All I can do is look at the broken pieces on the floor and in some crazy way that she has created within me, I think to myself how awful I was as a person. She got exactly what she wanted: to press enough buttons until I reacted and then ended up looking like the bad person. Her mission was successful!

The next several months continued to take its toll on my patience with Jessica's behavior toward me. My fuse was shortening. When I would be driving home from work or anywhere else, my anxiety would begin to build because I did not know which Jessica I would encounter when I walked through the door. If I would think it was going to be a "bad Jessica" night, I would be welcomed with warm compassionate woman. But "Doressica" confronted me frequently.

It was no secret that all four children had seen and sensed the tension that had taken place as of late. I was extremely concerned about them and wanted them to feel a warm loving household. In April, after Jessica was continually having altercations with Aspen along with numerous fights between the two of us, I received a call from my ex-wife expressing her concern about what she had been hearing from the kids. She asked me if we could sit down over lunch and discuss what was happening at my house. I agreed because I felt it was important that their mother know. I also knew that if Jessica found out that we were going to meet, she might flip out. But I did what was needed and best for the kids welfare.

Just as I expected, Jessica found out before I met my ex-wife and became enraged. She challenged me on why I was going to my ex about concerns. I told her that it was reasonable for a mother to be interested in the welfare of her children. Jessica was bilious to their mother's worries and said it was none of her business on what was taking place at our house. I could not believe my ears, because again, the flag was waiving that if it wasn't important to Jessica, no one should be concerned.

I met my ex-wife a few days later and we discussed everything. We had a very good relationship as co-parents and I felt no need to cherry coat the situation. She had been hearing information mainly from Aspen; I told her it was all true and agreed that all of her concerns were merited. She said that she had been thinking about the situation a lot and felt it might be good for the kids to stay over at her house for six weeks while Jessica and I worked on our issues. The first thing that popped into my head was I would not be able to see my kids for a month and a half, but knew that would be the best for the kids and agreed to her arrangement.

While driving home from lunch, I had mixed feelings on how Jessica might take the news. Though she preferred when my children were not around, I was inclined to believe she might blow a gasket since she had lost control in the decision making. As I walked in the door, I was met with coldness from Jessica along with a smart-ass tone and demands for an update on the conversation. I told her that we felt it would be good for Jeremy and Aspen to spend the next six weeks over at their mother's house and she erupted. She tried to say that my ex-wife and I had no right to make decisions about our kids. When I told Jessica I supported my ex-wife's point of view, I was met with more blistering remarks about my character and how I chose Tina over her. I was in a no win situation just like usual with this woman.

The kids staying at their mother's house didn't help Jessica and I. She continued her reprimands and interrogations about the decision even once it was already happening. She was a broken record that NEVER stopped! She denied we were having any problems and the kids needed to return home. When I clearly stated that we were having problems, ironically it made her pull out the verbal bullets and initiate a fight. All I could do is think to myself, *"Not having problems? Bullshit! What do you call this?"*

The kids returned at the beginning of April; however, there had been a lot of damage done to me and everyone under the roof. I felt torn apart inside and our marriage was still feeling strained. Jessica remained very bitter at both my ex-wife and me, reminding me about it any chance she got. Her foot was continually on the accelerator and seemly never ran out of gas. I was exhausted from the ridiculous amount of projectiles leaving Jessica's mouth.

After running to the grocery store one evening, I got back, poured myself a glass of wine along with a glass of water and starting preparing dinner like I did every night. About an hour passed when Jessica ask me where was the dish soap she had on the grocery list. I cringed inside because I realized I had forgotten the soap. And that's all it took... a simple oversight that in the big picture of life was meaningless.

For her, this forgetfulness was a tiny spark that just came in contact with a broken gas line. I stood there drinking a glass of water while she delivered blow after blow. She was standing about six feet away when I had reached the end of my rope. As she delivered one last blow at my character and called Tina a bitch, I reacted out of emotion and took what little was left in my glass and tossed the water into her face!

She immediately involved the kids by calling them downstairs, and manipulated them into eyewitnesses for her as she claimed she was the victim of (her own) tirade. She encouraged Ian to immediately call 911. The short story of both of our versions to different cops meant someone had to leave the house. I said I would leave since she did not have anywhere to go. I called Tina, explained the situation and asked her to pick up Aspen and Jeremy, then made arrangements to head to my parents, spending what would turn out to be several weeks. Within 24 hours of that incident, she filed a restraining order against me. I received the paperwork and saw how far she had stretched her story to the police, even saying she was afraid of me. (I can assure you Jessica is not afraid of anyone. She takes no BS from anybody and has no problem dishing it out.)

I wanted our marriage to work out, but was starting to lose faith. I resigned myself to living in my parents basement for the time being. My vow to Jessica was eternal, but I don't think God included people with BPD in the marital oath. Friends understood and invited me to hang out with them that coming weekend. Interestingly, though she filed the restraining order, her sense of abandonment kicked in and she called me Friday night. She started telling me how sorry she was for calling the police and wanted me to come home and make love to her. I was startled, but this was her method: push me over the edge and lure me back with sex.

My first thought was that she was setting me up to possibly be incarcerated. I felt like she was manipulating me even though I wasn't there, playing with my mind. Even though I was confused I wanted to be with the women I loved, so I headed home. I pressed the garage door opener and entered our bedroom, I slipped into bed where she laid and greeted me with a hug. She reassured me that she had made a big mistake and it would be corrected. We completed the night with wonderful sex and then fell asleep.

Little did I not know at the time, but my response to Jessica's emotional beat-down would cause me more shame, because calls where the police come out about domestic violence are taken very seriously. Yes, I said domestic violence! Any time police are called out where one spouse files an order of protection, a court date is automatically scheduled. It doesn't matter if it's throwing a paper towel or physically harming someone. In the eyes of the court, tossing a quarter filled of a glass of water at Jessica is comparable to husband beating up his wife. So, a few weeks later, both Jessica and I received separate letters in the mail stating that we were to appear in court, plaintiff and defendant (respectively).

I decided to call an attorney friend of mine and explain what took place. He felt comfortable that we could get the case dismissed as long as the case was assigned to one of the two judges that normally handled these types of cases. Unfortunately, it wasn't and we were unable to get the case reassigned; I ended up having the having to go in front of a judge that I knew (we attended college together). Talk about an embarrassment. Jessica, by law, had to meet with several people in private about what had been going on with our relationship — who knows what she said. When she came over and told me that everything was fine, I truly believed that she thought I had been scolded. Oh yes, we'd just be going home, my tail between my legs and grateful to her for "rescuing" me. My name was called on the docket, the judge looked at me oddly and then asked both Jessica and I what took place. The result was that I would be assigned to 12 weeks of anger management. I am stunned; Jessica is the one that needs it!

A few weeks later, my anger management class was filled with suspicious people and all I wanted to do is put my head between my knees. They went around the room, each person explaining everything from hitting his girlfriend to being involved in bar room and street fights. I was one of the last to go when I told them how my wife had been cutting me down about my decision to have the children stay with their mother, so I tossed a quarter filled glass of water at her. Several people chuckled and the guy next to me said, "No way you're in here for that?" The instructor lectured us about my water-throwing was an act of aggression and thus, we began the "management" process.

I spent the next 12 weeks attending and did my best in making it a positive experience. Withdrawing from a heated moment had not worked well in the past, but I figured I may have to do it repeatedly until it forced her demeanor to change. This experience was very damaging to me and Jessica knew it, but at least the name calling and cutting me down took a second seat for the next eight months. Whoever came up with cliché that "sticks and stones may break my bones but words will never hurt me" is full of crap and likely has never been married to a BPD.

81

One thing that stayed the same, however, was her intense drive and persistent way of pushing Jake to become the best wrestler he could be. With all of the time Jessica and Jake invested with practice and tournaments, he continued to be regarded as a formidable opponent on national rankings. We spent a lot of time and money traveling across the United States and I was (and am) very proud to see him reap the fruits of his labor. Jake's dedication to continue improving was exciting, though I was not quite sure what was fueling his zeal. I chose to believe he was devoted because he is in love with the sport and he was very gifted; however, I was concerned that Jessica's obsession with Jake's success may have caused him to potentially lose his desire to stay committed with the sport he loves so much.

Chapter 10

The Light Is Turned On

In July, we separated.

We had always had issues, but now people in the wrestling world became aware of our faults. She had confided to me that one of Jake's teammate's dads was willing to help move her out of my house and into Robyn's house. Not even marriage counseling had worked.

I was very hurt that Jessica moved out, but still wanted her to be my wife. I felt I had done everything I could yet I saw no hope. While separated, we continued going to therapy with little improvement. She had moved out and wasn't putting much effort into making things work, which was very frustrating to me. On several occasions, she would call at the last minute and would be late or unable to make the appointment.

I had tried a marriage counselor with my first wife, too. There is one thing I learned from the first marriage therapist: what are her actions telling you? Always judge by actions and not words. Jessica's actions were telling me that she was not 100% committed to our marriage and that was hard to swallow. Even though she was unreliable with our appointments, I made sure I went every time. In one particular appointment where Jessica was absent, the therapist brought to my attention that she thought that Jessica might display symptoms of Borderline Personality Disorder. That evening, I went home and looked on the internet. Holy Toledo, I could not believe what I read. It seemed like every website or blog I read fit Jessica perfectly.

I spent the next month coming home every evening and read anything and everything I could on BPD. I was astonished at how many spouses had encountered the same problems I had dealt with over the past several years. While reading everything I could in order to understand, I also didn't want Jessica to know about my researching (it would make her explode and destroy any change of returning to a functional marriage).

As usual, her "work drama" impacted our finances, which I still considered joint though we were separated. Her company was downsizing and her position was part of the cut backs. She did receive a six-month severance package, but my gut feeling hinted at what might happen. It did. Jessica called and asked if she could borrow some money. It wasn't a significant amount; if I didn't give it to her, she'd pick a fight and there would be less chance of reconciliation. I gave it to her because I was also concerned about Jake and Ian. She assured me she would repay me, which she did a few days later (and I was shocked).

By October, Jessica was putting very little effort into restoring the marriage. I felt the end was near. She was "enjoying her freedom" with friends and going out to bars. I continued to go to therapy to help ease my feelings about the marriage ending. Wrestling season had begun and she would be taking Jake to tournaments throughout the Midwest. That would fill her need for attention from the mostly male-dominated crowds and coaches.

I was doing my best to stay out of Jessica's business since I felt separation would be good for her. Then I found out that while she was at a national tournament, she was approached and "hit on" by a man who was a trainer for the United States Wrestling Team. This must have been a wonderful feeling for her because not only did she get the attention she so desperately loved, but also this guy was part of the national picture, putting her right at the epicenter of the wrestling circle. (I found that as I gave her space, the more she retreated.)

Immediately after meeting Luke (the national team trainer), Jessica's actions became very defensive towards both me and my family. In early November, I received a call from Jessica flying off the handle about how my mom came out to Ian's school to give him a birthday card. While she explained, I was blown away. I could not believe my ears, so I repeated, "You're upset with my mom because she dropped off a birthday card at school?"

I could not believe she was actually troubled about the fact of a step-grandmother giving a grandchild a birthday card. If anything, she should have been glad that my mother cared enough to put forth the effort. I did my best to pacify Jessica and let her know that my mom was only trying to do what was best for the children, trying to honor Ian's birthday.

By December, I knew Jessica and Luke were still talking as well as traveling to see one another. One thing I have learned through marriage therapy was that it is next to impossible rebuild a marriage when there is another person involved; however, I stayed the course and never mentioned anything about her and Luke.

With the New Year of 2011 came new hope and resolutions, and for me it is no exception. Sadly, January continued to be an extension of the previous year, with her flip-flopping between Luke and wanting our family back together. However, by mid-January, Jessica came to me, telling me that she has made up her mind and is committed to putting the family back together. She told me that is going to stop seeing and talking to Luke and focus on us, which makes me apprehensive but hopeful. At the end of our conversation she also told me that her severance pay is finished and may need some help until she gets a new job. (That's OK, you can say I am dumb... because I was.)

Although we are still separated and she was living with Robyn, Jessica and I started talking and meeting regularly. It appeared she was on board for reuniting. While visiting one evening, she told me that had made plans to go see Mike back in Chicago. He was going to be getting married in Las Vegas a few weeks later and she felt it would be nice to pay him and his fiancée a visit before their big day. I told her I thought that was a great idea. We spent the next two weeks focusing on spending more time together and took the rebuilding process day by day.

Since money was tight for her, she thought it would be best to drive. We only talked a few times on the phone while she was gone. On her first call, I asked how Mike was; she said he doing well and excited about the upcoming wedding. Shortly after getting off the phone, I happened to be on Facebook and for no reason in particular, I sent Mike a private message noticing he was online saying, "Congrats on the wedding and take care of my girl!" I never received a response, but didn't think much about it since he wasn't a big Facebook guy. I spoke one other time with Jessica during her trip and she told me she could not talk long; all of them were going out for dinner and she had to get ready.

She made it back into town Sunday. It was nice to not only see her, but also Ian and Jake. Little things kept happening that I thought were showing progress in her respecting me and relying on me, such as she called me when her car wouldn't start and asked for my help. It was rather cold so I handled everything outside while she stayed in Robyn's house. After getting it started, I sat in her car to make sure the battery got a good charge. I noticed a sheet of paper on the passenger seat showing the receipt for the oil change she had on her car the day before she left to drive to Chicago. I passively looked at the sheet and noticed the mileage on the paperwork was only about 75 miles lower than the current odometer.

It was at least 500 miles to Chicago one way. With a dazed looked in my face, I went into Robyn's house and I asked Jessica about the disparity in mileage. She paused for a moment and then told me she had actually ended up flying and did not want to tell me as I would be upset since she was low on money.

Jessica lying about something as petty as how she traveled seemed ridiculous. But because of her "training" me with her manipulative tactics, I could kind of understand since I had been helping her out financially from time to time while she was laid off. My biggest concern about the matter was she continued to lie, which left me feeling like I could not trust her. I did my best to explain my point of view and she apologized and promised to be truthful... again.

We continued to spend more and more time together, causing me to be hopeful about our future. The following Saturday, she asked if I would like to meet for lunch with her and the boys, which I gladly accepted. As she and Jake were already running some errands, she suggested I drop by and pick up Ian over at Robyn's house.

Ian opened the door and told me he was running a little behind. I told him to take your time and sat on the couch, looking at stuff on my phone. I noticed a legal pad sticking out of Jessica's briefcase. The front page appeared to be filled out completely almost like a letter, not bullet points for a job search.

My curiosity got the best of me and I pulled the pad out to discover a five pages letter. I got one sentence into the letter. "Dear Luke, I had an amazing weekend with you last weekend in Las Vegas..." I could hardly think straight, but I finished reading that letter. She was telling Luke how much she needed him in her life and how unhappy was in our marriage; reminding him about their sexual encounters that occurred between them. It hurt so badly! I told Ian that I had an emergency and ran out the door with the legal pad.

Fifteen minutes later, my phone rang and it was Jessica asking me why I didn't get Ian. I cleared my throat and told her that I knew she went with Luke to Vegas. Using her typical pattern, for several minutes she denied going to Vegas with Luke. I told her I saw the letter she wrote. She immediately changed erratic defense to forcefully striking back at me about reading her private things — again, trying to blame the actions on me instead of accepting responsibility herself.

When Jessica was in a corner, she used a stronger offense instead of a better defense. Finally, I had to cut her off and remind her it wasn't about blaming me, but her lying to me about where she went, who she was with, wanting to get back in the marriage. It all fell on her shoulders and I finally caught her in the act.

The following day, I scheduled an appointment with an attorney and moved forward with a divorce. I certainly had made my fair share of mistakes, but most of them were reactions from her criticizing or blaming me. If Jessica was not on board to mend our differences and make an attempt to make the marriage work, I believed I had no other alternative but to move on without her.

I met with the attorney and told her to file for divorce. Jessica and I did not talk much over the next few days, but I knew it would not be long for her to call and tell me she wanted us to get back together. I did everything I could while I was in her "wait before attracting him back" phase of her now well-known relationship manipulation cycle. I knew that when she perceived our marriage coming to an end that her "fear of abandonment" would kick in and motivate her toward immediate reconciliation.

At this point in our relationship, I knew I had to separate our finances. As I examined one statement, I saw where my card was being used to pay the balance off for her own individual account. She was using her credit card (that had a low credit limit of $1000 due to her bankruptcy) and then logged on to my account to pay the balance off on hers so she could spend more and help out her credit!

I just kept getting kicked time after time with her deceitful behavior. She kept taking advantage of me. I called her and said I needed to come over to talk. I told her what I had found, which she immediately denied. I knew I had to be direct with my comments, so I showed her the facts from the bank and told her that if I filed a claim of fraudulent actions that she would be guilty of a crime.

She went quiet for a few seconds and then tears started to roll down her eyes. Jessica looked up and told me because the severance package had run dry and was hurting for money. I zinged back about her needing extra money to go to Vegas. She admitted that was part of where her money went, but also was using some it for food. My own money was being used for them to frolic, party, sleep and have sex; it was far more painful than the money taken.

She admitted that I deserved someone far better than her. The room was so quiet as I just stood there thinking this was one of the first times I remember where she actually dug deep inside and decided to be honest with herself. With no barriers, her comment felt so refreshing, genuine and truthful. In some crazy way I found some comfort in Jessica's honesty. But I reminded myself why I was here. Stealing my credit cards was one thing, but to using it to fund spending time and have an affair was unbearable. (Dear God, why am I staying in this destructive marriage?)

I left Robyn's house. I wasn't sure if she was being genuine or if this was just another academy award winning performance. She had been caught stealing again and she was still unemployed with no source of income. I speculated the contrite behavior she displayed was to ensure I did not report the felony use of my credit card. Additionally, keeping me around for any potential need for money would help her get through the financial crisis. It was certainly in her best interest to make peace with me!

I took the next few days by myself to reflect on and ponder the future. There are countless reasons why I should move forward with the divorce papers that have already been set in motion; however, my heart continued my love for her.

Any normal person would have grown tired of the pain and constant unrest by now.

Jessica called me the next day (because of her own needs to take care of herself, not because she's worried about me), and I told her I was taking some time to myself. Her calls persisted for several days; I finally agreed to meet her. I know that she was going to make a significant effort in persuading me she was dedicated to fixing our marriage. I also know there is no possible way I can continue to go on with what I have dealt with the several years.

Of course, she was very apologetic, told me she loved me dearly and was ready to make our marriage work. Even though I was apprehensive, I so terribly wanted to think this was the time where the tide changed for our marriage. There would be rules; I demand her username as well as password to her email and cell phone accounts. Clearly, I no longer trusted Jessica.

She tried to get around it, but finally proceeded to give me her usernames and passwords. I found some assurance that she was cooperating by giving access to her cellular and email records, but then think to myself, *what is the value in a marriage if I felt compelled to monitor her every action?*

Over the next several weeks, she was on her best behavior and communicates with me several times a day, when she would express her love for me and the family. She told me she wants to move back into our house. It will only work if she is willing to work; she must make changes on her shortcomings. She told me she was going to work on the constant bitching, name calling and belittling.

A few weeks later, we decided to move her and the boys back into the house. For the next couple of weeks, she was extremely affectionate and in a happy mood and there was no complaining. But then she felt maybe we should get a new wedding ring to show a symbol of a new beginning. She seemed so happy, I agreed, though she did get a dig at me when she said she always struggled with the original ring. I thought the new symbol of matrimony would help us turn the corner. I am sure most of my friends and family felt I had a hole in my head when I told them that we were reuniting and she was moving back into the house.

Chapter 11

Drugs Don't Make It Better

Summer was approaching in 2011 and Jessica continued to be on her best behavior. I was hopeful that she had decided to make our marriage her top priority, but had my doubts considering her track record. The house was much more harmonious and I found less concern about what might flying out her mouth next. I am sure the children found it reassuring that there was a break from fighting along with Jessica showing more patience (did I just say patience and Jessica in the same sentence...WOW).

She was clearly more attentive my needs and appeared to being better with Aspen. I could tell Aspen was still unsure where her and her stepmother's relationship would be headed from day to day, but in the mean time, Jessica had implemented a ceasefire.

She was still unemployed for the first couple of months, but finally landed a sales job with a national laboratory that relieved some of the financial burden I was feeling. In the back of my mind, I was questioning if running out of money played a role in her decision to reconcile. I wasn't the only person who had that suspicion. Both my ex-wife and one of my closest friends confronted me with that as her only reason for apologizing. I heard what they were saying but chose to look past what I, too, suspected.

One other condition when she returned home (because I felt would be important for us getting back on track) was limiting the amount of "girl's times." She was excessively spending time with friends and not showing commitment to the family unit before the separation (not to mention all of the mistrust I went through with the Luke ordeal). Please don't get me wrong; I firmly believe it is important to spend time with your friends, but for now I believed it was more important to put the marriage over any of our friends. I was limiting my time with friends, too. Jessica agreed.

We spent the majority of our time with the kids, but when living with a BPD, you have to always be ready for the unexpected. Even though interactions were much better, I would regularly be faced with drama generally over the most minuscule thing. Her sharp and direct delivery was less malicious; therefore, I was able deal with the smaller speed bumps. Anything was better than what I had been through, leaving me with optimism.

I did my best to not bring up the past because I knew it was not healthy and will only set us back on any growth we have made. I had logged on and checked Jessica's email and phone calls shortly after she moved back into the house. There seemed to be nothing suspicious. However, several months after her return, the bad memories popped back in my mind. I did my best to purge the thought, but my curiosity took over and logged on into her cell phone records.

Disappointment hit my heart once again! As I scrolled through the hundreds of placed calls, there were eight entries for Luke's number — one call lasted 48 minutes. She had promised me that there would be no more communication with him.

I decided not to call her immediately and went to the gym to think about things. I concluded that if she really wanted things to work out then she wouldn't have jeopardized it by making contact with him. I finally got home and started cooking dinner, waiting for the right time to ask her about the phone calls. The kids got fed and go upstairs and that's when I told her I checked her cellular records, that I noticed there were several calls to Luke. She replied that she didn't appreciate I looked into everything she did. I reminded her that I had not looked at her emails or call records in months.

Like all the other times, she became defensive and tried to turn it around on me that I didn't trust her, that she didn't appreciate me monitoring her email and calls. I remind her that her behavior and lying subjected her to me checking to rebuild my trust. She came up with an excuse for calling Luke about Jake's ankle injury; I was enraged because he was a trainer, not a doctor. More excuses about leaving voicemails; I had to interrupt her at that point to tell her the problem again — she went against our agreement that was for our marriage and did it repeatedly.

More defensive moves and manipulative tactics. Promises. Loves me. Et cetera.

This was so old that I took a few hours to gather my thoughts. I let things slide again, but knew that she chose her needs over that of our relationship.

Not only is Jessica now involved with Jake's wrestling, but she's chosen to become very active with Ian's pursuit of football. This has her meeting and visiting with the high school coaches on a regularly basis. Every though Ian is not a stand-out player, I began to feel that there was more than just supporting the team while she rubbed shoulders with the male coaching staff.

She now had an even a greater need to be the center of attention than when we first met. There was a certain part of her that seems to always be in middle of all events. I realized that she only initiated helping or volunteering in any activity sports or work related events because it got her recognition and acceptance — none of it was because a group needs help. It also benefited her when she figures out a way to be in control of certain aspects of her "volunteer" groups, to gain more attention.

Even though Jessica's temperament had been significantly better since returning to the house, there were signs of her revisiting her old ways. Not only did she initiate countless arguments, but also began to feel justified to have her nights out with the girls. I was not opposed since she had really not spent much time with her friends, but little did I know that frequency was going to increase. Before long there were times where she would go out two or three times a week while I stayed at home with the kids. Back to old habits.

Unfortunately, hanging out at the bars with a squadron of ladies lends itself possible philandering if allowed. Often, Jessica would arrive home moderately intoxicated. Then she would explain to me in detail how one or several men approached her or friends and what was said to "blow them off." It is almost like she found some pleasure in talking about all the attention she received, and thought it showed she can go get another man. I can't get my head around it!

After she started going out again, I got a voicemail from my accountant asking me to give her a call immediately. After reviewing the monthly bank reconciliation, she noticed a few withdrawals that she couldn't place and was curious if I knew what they were. I asked the bank to check; these were electronic transfers from my company's checking account to my wife's personnel checking account. She did it again!

More excuses when I immediately confronted her. Her reason this time is we were low on money and says my money is her money. I remind her that business funds aren't for personal activities. She had the audacity to believe that she could more less hack into a bank account and take out money. I had to explain to my accountant what happened, which was embarrassing. More apologies to never do it again (I'd heard this before). I did my best to believe her.

But she was gravitating back to her old self. The belittling and arguing was as bad as it has ever been. She got intoxicated more frequently. She started a quarrel that she threatens to call the police. I started to feel that I could be blindsided by one of these antics and forced to leave my house if she decided to go through with her threat. Playing the "police" card was getting old and I felt that I had to watch my every move.

It's around this time that I stumbled across a couple of pill bottles in her nightstand — Adderall and Topamax. I was familiar with Adderall and found it surprising that would be something she needed because she didn't have ADHD. As far as the Topamax, I had no idea, and when I asked her she tells me it's a preventative drug to help her with migraines. (But she never had a problem with headaches.) I decided to go online later that night and while the drug was beneficial with migraines, it was also used to help mood swing patients.

It didn't take long for things to heat up again, and I decided that I should go to the police station and file an order of protection. I certainly did not want it to get to this stage, but with all the intimidation and emotional blackmail, I felt there was no other option. Sadly, I found myself playing along with the game that she started, yet felt this was the only way to equal the playing field.

When the "order of protection" paperwork came in the mail a week later, I was met with only a rage possible from Jessica. She hadn't done anything wrong so she was going out with friends.

After filing for divorce in late 2010 and not having it finalized since we had gotten back together, my attorney had been filing continuances. I had paid the entire amount for the divorce to my attorney and didn't want to have to turn around and pay the fees again. I guess I knew we were going to have to divorce even though I always wanted to believe that we could work things out with my heart. Jessica didn't know the paperwork was still filed and ready to go. I approached her and said we could have the divorce finalized.

She raised her head and with a hateful look in her eye, claiming to be puzzled because she didn't want a divorce; then she said she wanted it when the restraining order paper was opened. Then she claimed she was joking. I let it alone for a week, still confused. The holiday season was approaching and Jessica had been in good spirits. (Rule number one, if Jessica is in a good mood then I am in a good mood!)

Unfortunately with winter came wrestling, and so did Jessica's immersion with Jake's progress and training. Jessica took her focus to the next level. I was growing tired of this being her focal point. And the attorney told me that I really needed to make a decision about the divorce papers because the judge will likely cancel it at the end of the year; I told her to go ahead and cancel the paperwork.

Part of me felt relieved that this may be premonition that things were going to improve; however, Jessica had an extensive track record that the odds were stacked against me.

Chapter 12

The Last Chance

With Jessica in happy spirits and the cancellation of the divorce behind me, I was hopeful to get a fresh start on 2012. Granted, Jake was still wrestling and Jessica was obsessed with it more than ever. After explaining my concern about her losing focus on our relationship, she did a fair job of being more attentive to my needs.

Jake was entering the eighth grade and had caught the attention of the high school wrestling coaching staff. Because of his accomplishments, the head coach was eager to start working with him and invited Jake to start working out with the high school team. Both the high school team and head coach were well recognized for training high caliber athletes, so Jessica and Jake were excited about the invitation and considered it an honor.

The school year ended and there had not been major episodes from Jessica. Yes there was always some type of complaining, gossip or small cut down, but I had gotten used to it. Jim, the head coach, had taken a liking to Jake and he was constantly picking or dropping him off from practice. Jessica was appreciative of his help and they spent a lot of time talking and texting about Jake.

Jessica had always been overzealous about being involved with Jake's wrestling, but I found it rather strange that on a few occasions in the early evening she would drop whatever she was doing to run up to the high school to sign paperwork or enter him into a tournament. One other thing I found odd was how much information Jessica had received from Jim regarding the local wrestling scene about drug abuse or private home stories concerning previous wrestlers as well as parents of wrestlers.

In the back of my mind ran a concern of how could a high school teacher and coach divulge such private information. It should be private, particularly away from some mom of an up-and-coming star for his team. I could see that she, like always, enjoyed being deeply immersed in the all the scuttlebutt of people's lives. But we were nearing our one-year reconciliation and I ignored the little bell ringing in my head.

For some reason, once she started having more frequent contact with Jim the darker side of her personality had appeared again. I truly didn't know if I could make this relationship work. She kept doing whatever she wanted without any regard for me or my feelings. I didn't get it; there were so many discrepancies between her words and actions yet I continued to fight for my marriage.

I was losing faith that we could make this work. Unlike the past, I no longer got caught up in the heated arguments. Her detachment was different this time. Not only was she always out with her girlfriends, but she started hanging out with some mothers of high school athletes that were having affairs. I was not too happy about it, but kept my mouth shut. She seemed like it was no big deal and had a very carefree attitude about the company she kept.

In August, Jim invited Jake to go to Colorado in order to spend the week training at the Olympic Training Center. This was quite an honor for an eighth grader and he was very excited to be traveling with some of the upperclassmen.

Jessica made the decision to go, too, and spent a few days there before visiting one of her friends in Denver. She tried to make it sound like it is more about visiting her friend; however, it felt like it was more about hanging out the coaches.

When they were driving back from Colorado, she called to let me know that she was dropping off Jake to shower and get ready for a birthday party while she swung Jim to his house and would come back to then take Jake to the party. I thought that seemed odd. It was the first time where it just did not feel right. I knew Jim was married, but should I be concerned? Jessica had no respect for boundaries. I probably did not want to admit it to myself at the time, but now I realize it that the inevitable was drawing near.

Two weeks and the school years starts. I was doing all I could to stay strong. I wished Jessica would open her eyes to what she had done our marriage.

Ian played football for the high school team, but saw very little playing time, though we always went to support him. One Friday night game when the whole family was to go watch, Jessica told me that she and one of her fornicating wrestling mom friends were going to go up early and help out with a fundraiser before the game. I told her OK and I would bring up the rest of the kids.

After kickoff, I found her and immediately noticed she was intoxicated; her crappy attitude was in full force. I spent most of the time talking to friends and watching the game. I finally found her again well into the third quarter and before I could get a word out, she tore into me, accused me of talking bad about her to one of our mutual friends. I had no idea what she's saying. I wasn't sure she had any more to drink, but her intensity sure made me believe she had.

I told her I was heading home with the kids, and walked away. She continued to verbally sling mud. All I could think about was that she had lost her marbles. I heard the garage door go up around 11:30pm and drifted off to sleep once again. It wasn't until 1:00 a.m. that I woke to find that Jessica was not in bed, which I found strange. I hopped up out of bed, looked around the house and saw no signs of her. I knew she had to bring Ian home from the game so I went upstairs and found him sound asleep.

I reached for my phone and called her, only to get her voicemail. I called in 15 minutes only it go unanswered again. I got in my car and drove to the bars where she might be, but they all closed at 1:00 and it was nearing 2 am. I periodically called to see if she would answer. At 2:30 she answered her phone in a muffled voice, and asked, "What do you want?"

Thirty minutes later the garage door opened and she came upstairs. I demanded to know where she's been and she thinks I'm psychotic for asking. I tell her it's not unreasonable to ask where your wife is at 230 in the morning. She said they were at a bar. I told her I went there and they were closed at 1am. More excuses.

I tossed and turned most of the night with thoughts of what was my wife was doing until 2:30 in the morning. I couldn't deny that she could be having an affair given her recent behavior. At the end of the day it wasn't so much about her staying out so late, but how she did not communicate and did whatever she wanted with no consideration for what anyone else wanted.

I knew that I had reached the end of the road. She finally woke up mid-morning and I was met with little resistance as she laid in bed and we talked. I told her that I loved her very much but didn't feel like she treated me as number one. She agreed. I was rather shocked to hear her finally make sense. I told her that I thought we needed to file for divorce, and she agreed.

Ironically, that day was our anniversary.

I remembered feeling sad that my marriage had failed, but at the same time extremely relieved that I would no longer have to deal with the blaming, name calling, drama or moodiness she brought into my life. Jessica had been explaining our situation to a friend and said she was going to run over to her house to talk about moving in with her.

That was around 1:00 in the afternoon and she said she would be back shortly. Six hours had passed when I got a text telling me she had decided she and her friend were going out. I shouldn't have cared, but my heart was still in the game. As I dazed at the television, I reflected over the last eight years and all of the turmoil.

I went to the attorney a few days later and told her I was filing for divorce once again. The legal secretary was a personal friend and knew a lot of what I had been through; she looked over the top of her glasses with an "I told you so" expression.

Even with Jessica gone, I started receiving frequent calls and text telling me how much she loved me. Now it was different. I had already started taking back my identity unlike the times in the past when I just waited for her. I stood my ground when she tried reeling me back to her.

I knew that if I gave Jessica an inch that she would take a mile, so keeping her at arm's length was my best option of escaping this mess. I made an oath to never initiate contact, only to return her text or calls *when I had the time.* I would control the communications from my side of the line.

As our divorce drew near in late 2012, so did the amount of her attempting to communicate with me. Excuses for delaying the divorce were flooding my phone. She would attempt to make me jealous about dating a younger man. This spiteful side of her reassured me to press forward with the divorce.

It was a Friday right in the middle of the holiday season and I had opted out of going to the gym. Jeremy and Aspen were not home, so I was only cooking for myself. My phone rang and I noticed it was my attorney's number. I heard my friend's voice tell me that the judge had just finalized my divorce. The conversation was short and caught me off guard. I told her "Thank you" and "Happy New Year" then ended the call. The date is forever etched in my mind — December 28, 2012.

With the chicken sizzling on the stove, I gazed out the window reflecting on times Jessica and I spent together. If I think about the good times, I grow sad, so that night it was best that I looked back at all her drama, manipulation and deceit. It pulled me back to reality. I was filled with huge sense of relief that I was officially free of any her unstable and inconsistent behavior. My eyes begin to fill with tears as I raise my arms like a victorious athlete then yelled at the top of my lungs, "YES"!

Chapter 13

Incomplete Hail Mary

The new year arrived and with the divorce final, I was hopeful to start rebuilding myself and would ignore Jessica's calls or texts occasionally telling me how depressed or sad she was. I tried to do my best and stay the course. However, there were times that I fell short and allowed her back into my world — "Can I come over and see you" generally ended up meaning that we had sex.

Without a doubt, I do miss the laid back loving side of Jessica, the side where we lay in bed or on the sofa and I listen and hear no gossip or negative sentiments. I have strong feelings about there being an equal balance within a marriage and that was one of the many reasons I choose divorce. She no longer held that card so she was always on her best behavior.

Progress was slow. Admittedly the divorce was difficult on me. I didn't have boundaries on allowing her to call or text when she felt so inclined. In my heart I wanted to hear Jessica say that she realizes she made mistakes. Slowly, I do hold true to my word about never initiating communication with her.

My phone rang as I drove down the road. I could see it was her number and I answered the phone. She told me she wanted to talk about something; I was listening. With a regretful tone, Jessica admitted to me that she had been fooling around with one of the high school coaches. I immediately knew it was Jim.

She told me some details; it started while we were still married. I was very calm, but my heart took another blow. She was feeling guilty and wanted to admit what she had done. I tried to console her (Don't ask! I loved her!) and reminded her that he was married so she should stop. She began her old tricks and said he was pursuing her, blaming him for using Jake as a pawn to get with her. I hung up feeling sorry for her — people around town and wrestling community had their suspicions and would undoubtedly start talking about them.

About four weeks passed when she called again and asked to come over and talk. She arrived a short time later with tears in her eyes. Another trick in her book trying to get a reaction. That would be exactly what she wanted. This was no longer about her and she didn't know how to cope with the loss of control.

She sat in a chair, trying to bait me by asking if I'd had an affair. No and why? She said she had been to the doctor and was told she had bladder cancer, which may have been passed through a sexual partner. She insinuated that if I had sex with someone that it could have been passed on to her. I assured her that I had only been with one person while being married and that was her.

The way I saw it (while she was trying to bait me), this meant that Jessica had an intense amount of guilt and was hoping she could somehow be able to rationalize it by blaming me. Since I wasn't an adulterer, it did not work. In a matter-of-fact way, she quickly suggested that it could of happened several other ways and not to worry.

Turning to another one of her tricks, she then stared telling me how sorry she was for tearing our marriage and family apart. She began begging to know if there was anything she could do to put our marriage back together. I told her that her appeal to me to get back together was centered around her wants rather than our marriage.

Feeling strong and as if I had actually moved further down the path of healing than I realized, I also mentioned that I thought it would be good for her to look getting help for people with board line personality disorder and felt she could benefit from therapy.

She didn't seem warm to the idea, but then suggested we go to a therapist together. She knew she could not be pushy like she normally was or I would shut down. I simply said I'd considerer it. She walked out the door and promised she'd do whatever it took. I told her to have a good night and I would think about it.

After a few days of contemplating, I decided that throwing a "Hail Mary" was worth a final shot, but told Jessica that it would be her responsibility to schedule the appointments. I felt that I had given much more than she had in working on our relationship; I needed to see that she was actually committed to piecing things back together. Jessica said that she had no problem in setting up the appointment and called back later that evening to let me know what time we would be meeting the following week.

We spent the next couple months going to see the therapist once a week. At times, I felt like there was hope that Jessica might be a glimmer of hope for reconciliation. Unfortunately, it only took a few days before I was reassured that washing my hands and finalizing the divorce was the right thing to do.

There seemed to be little progress on Jessica's part while in therapy. Trying to rekindle the flame is often difficult for a couple to do. I was definitely not willing to jump back into the turbulent relationship I had endured for six years; clearly, Jessica was not willing look inward and work on the areas that had hindered her for so many years.

A few weeks passed and we had not been back to therapy. It appeared that last effort for piecing things back together was finished, too. My phone rang and it was Jessica with a very agitated voice asking if she could come over and talk with me. I told her that would be fine.

Next verse, same as all the others. She showed up at the front door with tears in her eyes. After sitting down she starting crying frantically and told me how upset she was with herself for getting involved with Jim along with sharing that Ian heard all about it at school. She took a couple seconds to gather herself and then asked me to take care of Ian and Jake if she died or killed herself.

Frankly, I was not shocked by her statement, but knew that any time someone talks about suicide it is a serious issue, so I did my best to console her and assure her everything would be alright. I had seen all the ways that Jessica could manipulate or use emotional blackmail, but felt that her talk of suicide was likely more of a cry for help. Even though her mention of suicide did not surprise me, I felt very sad for Jessica that she had resorted so low in using a tactic to guilt me into being so concerned for her welfare attempting to suck me back into the relationship.

I talked her off the ledge and sent her home, with our interactions happening at less frequent intervals after that episode. From time to time she would call, mainly when she had been drinking would call up wanting a booty call or looking for sympathy. When I told her we shouldn't have sex, Jessica saw it as being rejected and would sometime show up on the doorstep anyway. Jessica definitely did not like the fact that I had rejected her physically.

The last night she tried to get me to sleep with her is when I believe Jessica finally came to the realization that our relationship had come to an end. I had distanced myself far away from her allure of seduction and broke through the web of mistrust, lying and manipulation.

Chapter 14

What I Learned

Without question, my six years married to Jessica were the most turbulent of my life. My sole purpose for writing this book was because I felt the need to help others who had gone a through similar relationship, to point out episodes that may help them see their own relationships before it gets to the point where mine did with Jessica. If you are currently in or recently finished being with someone with BPD, my heart goes out to you — it's not because they are a bad person, but because I truly know the pain and heartache you are going through.

I am sure you have had a myriad of incidents that left you scratching your head wondering want the hell is going on and why are you still in this relationship. The answer is because you love the person. You remember all of the great times and often live in those moments while simultaneously lose your own identity; you start not liking the person you have become. I often say that in the beginning Jessica made me a better person, but at the end I was worse-off.

There are things that you can recognize and learn from your relationship, both in identifying those red flags as well as how to keep yourself strong and true to your beliefs. Over the years, I noted there were quite a few flags. Now, I've been able to consider their causes, the outcomes and what I hope you'll be able to use sooner rather than later.

First and foremost, if you believe your partner has BPD, gently encourage them to get help through therapy. If they agree, then I wish you the best and hope you make the relationship work. There is nothing more wonderful than when two people work together to make a healthy relationship. You may still have some of the highs and lows as most relationships have, but if both people (especially the BPD partner) are dedicated then anything is possible. Unfortunately it is not uncommon for people with BPD to resist any type of therapy; if this is the case, get ready for some stormy weather followed by periods of calm waters then gale force winds once again. You will need help and I encourage you to find support groups or therapy for yourself.

Understanding the BPD's early childhood years can help you offset trigger moments For instance, I learned that since Jessica was born, she was forced to claw and fight for everything she got. This fostered her nature to be a tenacious unrelenting individual. There are an infinite amount of times where she would banter with the attempt of devaluing how I felt, which was totally irrelevant to the situation at hand but was how she handled stressors from an early age. Her personality was created by two unloving parents that constantly complained and talked badly towards her, illustrating to her by example that was the correct way to cope. Because of her passion and persuasive manner were honed over many years, there were times where she was successful and I began to second guess my inner feelings. Her use of manipulation with me was paramount throughout the entire relationship.

One area where I failed in the relations (and would be of great benefit for the non-BPD partner to use when episodes flair) is do as much research and reading about how to communicate with you BPD partner when they are having emotional issues. It is important to realize that it is just as difficult for the BPD as it is their companion. I always felt as if I had to be defensive about comments or attacks. Standing your ground and having boundaries is extremely important to the BDP; as long as they know the "rules" you set forth, things can be managed more effectively and in a more healthy manner.

Knowing what I do now, it's apparent that I should have done a better job of being more calm and biting my tongue at various antics. This is easier said than done when you are being called names, hearing lies or being manipulated. It takes a big person to sit back, take bullets and not fire back. Verbal attacks from BPDs are common, and the last thing you should do is argue in return (even if you are right). This "lack of correction" concept is best explained in Paul Mason and Randi Kreger's Book, "Stop Walking on Eggshells," when they say:

> If the BP knows that the button-pushing is having the desired effect—whether consciously or unconsciously—chances are that the behavior will be repeated.

I lived this repeatedly in my BPD relationship; it was almost as if my BPD partner enjoyed arguing! It was a way of life for her. If I did not argue, she would continue pressing my buttons until she got her desire response. For the non-BPD partner, this is a double-edged sword. If you take a stand and do not argue, the jabs keep coming; arguing back gives the BPD what they want, but ultimately makes you start second guessing why you are in the relationship. Either way, you lose in the eyes of the BPD and ultimately doubt yourself.

Another commonality in BPD individuals is "gaslighting." I was completely unaware of the term until I started learning about her probably disorder and how I could work with it and her better. Gaslighting is a form of psychological abuse in which a victim is convincingly manipulated into doubting their own memory, perception, and sanity; it was used against this BPD individual previously, thus it is used by them ongoing and usually without their partner's awareness. In my relationship, she would try to change the facts or highlight things that didn't really happen (such as my misplaced credit card was really a moment of permission for her to use it that never took place). The presentation of information was supposed to make me think I "was losing it," thus giving control to the BPD.

This need for redirecting fault also links with a BPD's tendency to blame others for their own pains, because they likely heard blame placed on the "missing partner" in the home while younger and they don't have to deal with any accountability of their own. When something doesn't go right, it is always appropriate (in their mind) to aim blame anywhere but themselves. at me or someone else. Blaming can be a daily occurrence, reaching the point where you may just take the blows. It doesn't matter how small or extreme the finger pointing may be, the toll of blame cuts deep into how the non-BPD partners saw himself or herself.

When these fights and confusing events occur, you likely will convince yourself that this is not the relationship for you. But you also realize a pattern has formed; the BPD will suck you right back into his or her web of chaos. This action is what they call "hoovering" (yes, like the vacuum) and at the time, I did not know that is actually a term for the push/pull tactics. Many BDPs may use this mechanism; my entire marriage was filled with this undesirable behavior. A BDP will promise change or give false hope, then sucks you back into the same cycle of pushing and pulling.

This tactic is closely related to the Borderline's fear of abandonment. When you have been pushed or pulled extensively and are ready to walk away, the BPD will assure you things would change, show compassion and even offer sex to suck you right back into the relationship so they are not alone. Hoovering and attachments are about their needs, not yours.

I could never put my finger on the pushiness or short fuse, particularly around discussion of getting married or our wedding. Shari Schreiber front an article, "Til death do us part," and she gives an accurate account that may explain the BPD perspective on marriage:

> You must try to wrap your head around the fact that Borderlines do not treat marriage as a new beginning--but rather, an end-game. All their seductive behaviors, their caregiving and affection, their understanding about you and your needs, come to a fairly abrupt halt once you've tied the knot. That sexy Siren you've fallen for could literally shut down the candy store, once she's secured this relationship.

There is one question that needs to be asked for anyone who is dating or considering marrying a potential BDP: "Are you willing to spend the rest of your life in a relationship that is an "emotional roller-coaster?" If your partner is actually BPD and is not willing to work on it with therapy, you will have wonderful experiences followed by excruciating painful times; you will question why you are in that relationship. Far be it from me to throw stones in glasses houses, I filed for divorce two times in six years and lived in my parents basement each time. In spite of your feelings _in_ the relationship, it could be the feeling of "relationship" rather than the holistic attachment with that partner. If he or she does not get help, I assure you that you will be looking back down the road dismayed asking yourself why you stayed so long in the relationship.

One comment in therapy was very insightful. The therapist told me that she was the type of person that needed multiple men in her life. More male friends than female, attention-seeking behaviors, promiscuity — it makes more sense now that I understand more of the BPF mindset. There are several studies, including one by Texas Christian University, providing evidence where daughters that grew up with the absence of a father (and his love) are more likely to engage in riskier more promiscuous sex than others with a nurturing father figure. Combine that with the neglect from the remaining female figure(s) and the need for affection fuels the indiscriminate need for male attention.

My take on the need for many men stems from a BPD's desire to fill the void left by an absentee father (likewise, a BPD who seeks to replace a forgone mother). It goes back to the first point in this chapter - the early years of childhood help form our personality, our beliefs and images of role models (correct behaviors). In this case, the absent male figure in her life meant she was always hunting to fill all the voids left by him. Shallow acceptance from men leaves her feeling desired and beautiful, things missing from a father figure. It's quantity of contacts, not quality for a BPD!

Something I didn't experience was the BPD inflicting harm on him/herself. My experience was all outward emotional lashings, but some BDP will use a sharp object (such a razor or knife) to cause self-harm as a way to relieve the mental pain or to control the feeling of a "rush." Personally I think it is a way to forget about all the pain they have endured. If you have had a horrible headache for several days and I hit you as hard as I can in your stomach there is a really good chance you are going to forget about the massive headache you currently have. Maybe it's not cutting but piercings, tattoos or other actions that may occur when the BPD feels at a low-emotional point, taking the mind off of one kind of pain and focusing it somewhere else.

As I look back now the only person I blame is myself. The first three years after the divorce, I was more upset with myself than with her. I get mad at myself for staying in the relationship as long as I did. It pains me at times to think back about how she treated Aspen. I am slowly healing from the torment and know that it will make me a better person. At the same time, I think about many of great times we had together — I also identify how often these wonderful times deteriorated quickly into mood swings.

It has now been close to four years since the divorce and thought it would be best to heal and work on myself before possibly dating. I have been out on a handful of dates over the past six months and one of the first things out of my mouth when I am talking with them is, "Tell me about your relationship with your parents." Look, I know that there are many people that may not have good rapport with their parents, but I am not willing to take a chance ever again.

While I was writing this book and reflecting on the whole process and flags and my own actions, I see now that I recognized to some extent that my BPD was unable to love the way I knew it, yet I expected her to behave as I had learned the world to function. She didn't have that frame of reference. I believe strongly in unconditional love and feel that this is something she was unable to do. Quite frankly, I am still unsure to this day how she views love. Again, Schreiber has worked with many BPD individuals and help me when she wrote "What's love got to do with it":

Love is an abstract concept for somebody with BPD—and its associated with pain. The Borderline's yearning for love is experienced as dramatic, painful emotions that were confused with affection for an unresponsive/unavailable parent during childhood, that constituted unrequited (or un-returned) love.

Reliving certain moments while working on this book were, at times, very painful. If it only helps one person then my efforts were worth the trouble. Not all relationships can overcome unhealthy actions, erratic mood swings and other relationship-busting actions, no matter how hard you may try. There may come a time that you must be willing to accept the fact that you have done everything you can and move on with your life. This will most likely be difficult as is any divorce or breakup, as I have shared, but I can assure you over the long journey of life that you will save yourself a lot of pain, heartache and self-worth.

I would like to think that there are successful relationships of couples who have a BPD partner. I want to believe there are many stories of stormy relationships yielding "sunny skies" — I have the upmost respect for those people in that relationship. It takes a lot of effort for the BPD to take accountability by working on themselves through therapy as it does for the partner who continually must learn how to deal with their partner's unpredictable behavior. For those putting forth the hard work, I hope that you find success with your relationship which grows into a life of happiness. As with anything, there will be peaks and valleys, but hopefully you can assure your partner that you will be by their side helping him or her every way you can. Remember to develop boundaries in order to keep your sanity (and it helps them control their processing, too).

If by chance you are a BPD, please understand that your marriage or relationship is a two way street; it is important for you to realize that your actions have major impacts on your non-BPD partner. For example, it is extremely puzzling when your words are not supported by your actions, particularly when there are facts that don't align with your story. The rollercoaster of emotions and outburst weighs just as heavily on your partner as it does you.

Good luck and I hope you find happiness!

About the Author

Berkeley Carson is the owner of a graphic arts company, helping businesses for close to 30 years. He received his undergraduate degree in Psychology and Business Administration from a liberal art college in Iowa.

After significant research, he recognized that there was a need in sharing his story in order to help others who have encountered struggles with their BPD relationship. He felt that the voice of many partners of the BPD was often misunderstood and unbelievable. His strong feelings of family values is what led him to letting other partners know that they are not alone.

He still resides in Kansas City with his two children, Jeremy and Aspen. Jeremy is now a freshman in college and Aspen is a junior in high school. He still remains active in Ian and Jake's life.